# I Kicked Out On Two
## The Education of a Wrestler

by

Bobby Blaze Smedley

# Twenty Seventh Street Books
Ashland, Kentucky
© 2016 Robert Lee Smedley
All Rights Reserved
ISBN-13: 978-1-5375-3564-7
ISBN-10: 1-5375-3564-1

*Cover Photo by Tom Worden*

# ❧ Foreword by Matt Wolfe ☙

"So, you think you can fucking do it?"

"Huh?"

"You think you can fucking do it?"

This was the first conversation I ever had with Bobby Blaze. I was attending a wrestling show in Winfield, West Virginia with my friend Kris Brown. The show was being promoted by Bobby, and had many great stars on it. Kris and I never missed a chance to attend a wrestling show and heckle to our hearts content. This night was no exception. During intermission I was walking by Bobby's "gimmick table" when he stopped me and we had the conversation I mentioned earlier. I didn't know it at the time, but that conversation would lead to some of the greatest times of my life. That night I left Winfield with Bobby's number and email address and an invitation to "get a hold of him when I thought I could do it." The following week, I emailed him and made plans to start training to become a professional wrestler. Through that summer Bobby taught me many valuable lessons not only for the ring, but for life as well. He taught me respect; discipline, professionalism and how to take pride in my work, not to mention a Cornish hype (look it up).

Cary Grant said, "Probably no greater honor can come to any man than the respect of his colleagues." If that's true then Bobby should be overflowing with honor, for he is truly respected by his peers. I've seen it many times. Whether it was WWE referee Charles Robinson and Scott Armstrong arranging for Bobby to come visit while they were in town, or Kane and Dustin Rhodes taking time to make sure they stopped and had a chat with him. I once mentioned to Vampiro how much I had enjoyed a match between him and Bobby and he told me "Bobby is an amazing person; he really carried me that night." I've heard Kevin Sullivan, Bobby Fulton, and The Rock N Roll Express all talk about how much respect they have for Bobby, and that's just to name a few. Jim Cornette even wrote the foreword for his first book! (If you didn't know that, then buy the damn book!)

Bobby is truly one of a kind. Sure, he's blunt but he's also honest. He would do anything for anyone without a second thought. He's done more for me than I can ever thank him for. I love him like a father and respect him like no other. To put it short and sweet, Bobby is the fucking man. You may not know that now, but I promise you will by the end of this book. Enjoy!

By the way Bobby, yea, I do think I can fucking do it, ya prick!

Matt Wolfe, a.k.a: Shane Storm

I first met Bobby "Blaze" Smedley in January of 2003. My nephew Tom had recently brought home a flyer from a local wresting show he had attended and passed it along to me. The flyer was an advertisement for a wrestling training school being run by Bobby Blaze. I was already familiar with Bobby from his work in World Championship Wrestling and Smoky Mountain Wrestling and knew he was the real deal. In addition, a couple of Tom's classmates, Matt Wolfe and Kris Brown had begun training with Bobby and spoke very highly of the experience.

I've been a fan of professional wrestling since I was very young and had always nurtured a dream of possibly getting into the sport myself one day. So when I woke up dreadfully hung over on New Year's Day 2003, and while looking for something else entirely I came across Bobby's flyer instead, I told myself that it was no coincidence. It was Fate trying to get my attention.

"Call the man," I said to the bleary eyed figure in the mirror. "If you don't, you'll be wondering 'what if' for the rest of your life."

The timing was right as far as where I was in my life was concerned. Recently divorced, recently unemployed, I certainly had the free time not to mention the attitude. I was by no means young (to put it in perspective, I graduated high school with the father of fellow trainee Kris Brown) but on the other hand I sure wasn't getting any younger. So after medicating with hair of the dog the rest of that day I called the number on the flyer the next morning.

My call was answered by a voice I recognized from his many Smoky Mountain promos– "Candido, you son of a bitch!" Bobby was polite but also very no–nonsense. "Bill, I'd be happy to train you if you're serious. If you're not, please don't waste my time or yours." I appreciated his candor. Being indeed serious I made arrangements to meet Bobby the following day in Ashland.

I'll admit to being a little star struck the next morning as this guy I'd seen wrestling on television so many times (he pinned Jerry Lawler for Christ's sake) pulled up next to my car and had me follow him to the building where he had his training ring set up. I'd have to say that Bobby is too genuine and down to earth for anyone to remain in awe of him for long however. Since that day I've been very proud and honored to call Bobby my friend.

Bobby's training was grueling and thorough, though I'm sure nothing like what he went through at the Malenko School. Bobby taught us not just the moves and holds (correctly, I might add), he taught us how to work, how to put together a match that made sense, that wasn't just a string of stupid high spots. He instilled respect in those of us who stuck with it, respect for the profession, respect for yourself and your opponent, respect for the match. How many wrestlers do you see these days who wipe their boots off before they get into the ring? Bobby's trainees do, just like he himself did.

Bobby's name carried similar respect in every locker room I was ever in. In fact, when I was first starting out I got a lot of bookings after answering a single question.

"Who trained you?"

"Bobby Blaze."

"When can you start?"

Matt Wolfe, who wrestles as Shane Storm, and I have been in the ring together literally hundreds of times, either tagging together or working against one another and I'll bet there hasn't been more than a handful of those matches where at one time or another one of us hasn't remarked on how fortunate and thankful we are that we had the opportunity to be trained by and become friends with Bobby.

I'm certain in my case that I would never have had anything like the career I've had as an independent wrestler (almost seven hundred matches including two tours of Mexico) if I hadn't been brought into the business the right way by Bobby. I owe him a lot.

None of which, of course, is any reason why you should buy this book. I just wanted to let the world know in print how much I think of the man.

No, why you should buy this book is because it's a damn good read. Some of the stories are funny, some inspirational, some educational or even philosophical. Every one of them is totally entertaining. Bobby is a natural-born storyteller and his voice comes through loud and clear in this book, as well as in his first one, *Pin Me, Pay Me*, which I strongly suggest you pick up if you haven't done so already.

If you ever wanted to sit down next to an old school wrestler who has been there and done that all over the world and listen as he tells you one great story after another, this book is about as close as it gets. Enjoy, my friends.

William Bitner, a.k.a: DFZ

*Shane Storm and Death Falcon Zero, The Death Stars*

# Table of Contents

### ❧ One ☙

*"Upon the plains of hesitation bleached the bones of countless millions, who on the threshold of victory sat to wait, and while waiting, they died."*

### ❧ Two ☙

*"Is there anyone so wise as to learn by the experience of others?"—Voltaire*

### ❧ Three ☙

*"The quality of any advice anybody has to offer has to be judged against the quality of life they actually lived." Douglas Adams*

### ❧ Four ☙

*"Lifestyles of the rich and the famous, They're always complainin', Always complainin' If money is such a problem..."—Good Charlotte*

### ❧ Five ☙

*"Tryin' to make a livin' and doing the best I can...and when it's time for leavin' I hope you'll understand, I was born a ramblin' man."—The Allman Brothers Band*

### ❧ Six ☙
### ❧ Yard Time ☙

*"Ask a group of school children what they want to be when they grow up and not one will say: 'I want to be a screw and look after tattooed psychopaths in a cold damp prison.'" Mark Chopper Read*

## ❧ Seven ❧

*"The greatest hold in professional wrestling is the hold it has on its fans."*

## ❧ Eight ❧

*"Friendship... is not something you learn in school. But if you haven't learned the meaning of friendship, you really haven't learned anything."—Muhammad Ali*

## ❧ Nine ❧

*"Whenever I think of the past, it brings back so many memories."—Steven Wright*

## ❧ Ten ❧

*"Give me chastity and continence, but not yet."
St. Augustine*

## ❧ Eleven ❧

*"Always go to other people's funerals; otherwise they won't come to yours."—Yogi Berra*

## ❧ Twelve ❧

*"Here is the test to find whether your mission on Earth is finished: If you're alive, it isn't."—Richard Bach*

## ❧ Thirteen ❧

*"I don't care if the average guy on the street really knows what I'm like, as long as he knows I'm not really a mean, vicious guy. My friends and family know what I'm really like. That's what's important."—Don Rickles*

# ᪥ Preface ᪥

"1, 2…" and right when the ref's hand was about to strike the canvas, out of desperation I grunt and thrust my hips up hard. Thrusting, I wasn't merely trying to escape an attempted pin, I was trying to survive. I jerked and thrashed my shoulders up off the wrestling mat to kick out of the pin, escaping a loss in the squared circle. Not only was I trying to escape being defeated, I was trying to get away from the grizzled wrestling vet that had been trying to teach me a lesson in respect. Respect is a lesson one must learn early on if you ever want to make it in professional wrestling. I was learning that lesson first hand and fast. I was also kicking out! Shoulders up just in time, I had just kicked out on two.

"Damn, that was close," I thought to myself. Out of the corner of my eye I could see the referee pointing to the time keeper and then to the excited crowd indicating as he waved his fingers, "Two! Only a two count." Rapidly blinking my eyes, a man in black wrestling tights and his face painted like that of the devil was advancing quickly towards me as I reached for the rope. I tried to pull myself up just in time to get out of this maniac's way. What an opponent! I move! He hits the turnbuckle full force before staggering backwards into the middle of the ring. "Bobby, Bobby, Bobby…" the fans chanted my name. I knew it was time for me to begin making my comeback. "By god, I didn't just kick out on two, I'm gonna win this match!" Spin Kick, Dropkick, I go for a quick pin, and when he kicks out, "Bam!" right when he gets up, I hit him with my Northern Lights Suplex. One, two, three! "Thank you brother," is whispered under my breath. "And your winner, Bobby Blaze!!!"

That's what I do, I kick out on two. Sure, I've been pinned and I've been paid, but I also learned how to kick out on two. I had kicked out on two my entire life. I had to overcome many obstacles just to break into the business, let alone have a quality match with someone. It's a tough business if you really want to make it, but I was determined that I would make it, and I did. I had always wanted to be a wrestler, a professional wrestler. I knew this at an early age and set my goals on doing so. Did I want to be a wrestling star? No, I just wanted to be a wrestler. I wanted to be a pro, and a pro I was. I also wanted to make money. First you learn to work, and then you learn to make money, that's what I had always heard. So, I learned to work. I also learned what it meant and what it took, sometimes the hard way, to be a professional. In every aspect of the wrestling business, I tried to be a complete professional. I wanted to learn to wrestle, work, and to have the respect of my peers. I could give a damn about what others may call, "Sports Entertainment," I am a professional wrestler. This is what I do. This is what I chose to do for a living. This is what I have been trained to do. I kick out on two!!! So this is my story...and one thing just led to another...

*I Kicked Out On Two, The Education of a Wrestler*

# ❧ Introduction ❧

There's a lot more to Bobby Blaze Smedley than meets the eye. If you've read, *Pin Me Pay Me, Have Boots Will Travel* then it probably feels like you already know him. You probably think you have a good idea about who he is or what he's all about. But there's so much more about Bobby than what's in just one book.

The response to Blaze's first book has been well received. Known throughout the world for his days in professional wrestling as a former Smoky Mountain Heavyweight Champion as well as worldwide television exposure on World Championship Wrestling and the more recent WWE Network, Blaze seems hotter than ever. Now he's back with even more fascinating stories told through his unique story-telling style that makes for a fun, heart-felt read for everyone. You don't have to be a fan of professional wrestling to enjoy his stories.

Blaze slowly learned the valuable lesson of not letting the wrestling business use him, but rather learning to use the wrestling business to his benefit, Blaze brings even more insightfulness from his world and into his life after professional wrestling with his second memoir, *I Kicked Out On Two, The Education of a Wrestler*.

Bobby Blaze Smedley: If you read my first book, I appreciate it. I'll go ahead and put this out there for you if you did read it: there may be some things repeated here, but that's just the way my mind works. I can assure you that you will still enjoy this book and these stories as much as you did in the first one.

I can also assure you that every single thing in this book, as goofy or unrealistic as it may seem, did actually happen. Well, I at least think they happened. I mean, I was there after all, at least for most of it. Yes, I've had my moments of clarity, and many more that weren't so clear. Nonetheless, I'll tell you now, these things are all true, and they are as real as professional wrestling. It's all real to me dammit! I should know I was there; I lived them, and lived to tell about it.

Just so you know up front, this book does contain adult language. I use awful language at times. I write a lot like I talk. You'll hear my voice coming through as you read it, especially if you know me. And, whether I'm talking or writing, I use adult language. That's just the way I am. That's the way it is. I don't do it for shock value. I don't do it without purpose; I do it to get my point across. I have used cuss words since I was ten years old, so I doubt I'll stop using bad words anytime soon. Here's your second warning: This book contains adult language!

Now that we have that out of the way, "Onwards and Upwards," that's what I always say, or at least I said it once, or maybe I thought I said it. Here's one more warning. If you're looking to read a book about or from some corporate sports entertainment bullshit that's a part of a story line, then, this book might not be for you.

Why another book? Well, that's simple. I need the money. It's not like I got rich off the first one. Seriously, I have so much more to say and so many more stories to tell. I've had people ask me for more stories, wanting more details about traveling to other countries, or about what it's like to be on television. Many wanted to know more details about some certain things I mentioned in the other one. People want to know about whom I wrestled and if I know certain wrestlers. This is especially true when a wrestler dies. Sadly, I've known far too many that have and I'll fill you in on that in this book as well.

I've even had people tell me I should write a book. Well, "I did" is what I tell them. I guess they were too damned cheap to buy it. (Oh by the way, it's still available on Amazon at amazon.com/author/bobbyblaze Cheap Plug!) Then, if they've read it, they say, "Well, you should write another one." So, here's another book.

Anyway...on with the show.

# ❧ One ❧

*"Upon the plains of hesitation bleached the bones of countless millions*

*who on the threshold of victory sat to wait, and while waiting, they died."*

## ❧ A Pro Wrestlers Love Letter ❧

I've loved you forever! Even when I have tried to walk away from you, you pulled me back to you. You're such a slut, yet I still desired you. You sold yourself like a cheap whore, and I paid. I wanted you so bad! I paid! From the first time that I paid, just for a chance to see, just to be around you, I paid! Before I even saw you in person or met you personally, I knew I loved you. I had watched you from afar and finally saw you in person and I fell even further in love with you. I got my chance to see you up close and in person, and I just knew. I knew I just had to be close to you. I even learned to sneak through your back door without paying you. I did it because I knew. I knew one way or another I was going to be with you. Call it infatuation! Call it lust! Call it love! I was going to cop a quick feel, just to see you. You bitch! You became my mistress! I know others that had loved you and had been where I was going, yet I wanted to still be with you. When I kissed you, you bit me. Your bite was like that of pure lust, and I loved it. Passion!

When you broke my heart, I came running back into your arms, forgiving you, my desire to only see you, my mistress. You little bitch, you went to another town, many towns and cities where others were willing to pay to see and be around you just as I had. But, when you came back, I was so forgiving, and I took you right back with open arms, aroused, excited, and with even more lust and love for you. When I first entered you, I was so young, so innocent, so naive, yet it just felt so right. Pure Pleasure! Then there was pain, yet you were worth it. Now, after years of your mental and physical abuse, you drag me back to you, asking forgiveness from a body that can't forgive, from a mind that can't forget, yet I gladly take you back. I walk away, I break up, and you just don't get it. You think we are still together,

1

because you know I love you unconditionally. It's true, I do! The sleepless nights driving home from being around you. The pain and the sleepless nights from a shoulder that is tender to the touch. My neck, tight and sore, will never permit a full night's sleep as I will stay up for you. My back wrecked from the nights that you didn't care how hard I fell for you. My knees weak, the pain, from bone on bone contact. I crawl out of bed, because I know you await me and in order to see you, I have to hit the road or catch that early flight just so I could be in you one more time. Maybe I whored myself out and you were just my love, my mistress, it didn't matter, I was going to be there for you, no matter how bad I hurt, no matter my pain, no matter where you were I would be there for you. I loved you then, and I love you now, because, I just cannot let you go. As many times as I have tried to break this thing off, you've pulled me back.

*The author, Bobby Blaze, passing out a little advice to the boys.*

My heart pumps faster, yet it aches, my adrenaline accelerates, even though my body has slowed down, whenever I hear you're near, those feelings come back one more time. I have to stay, and I'll stay a little bit longer than any of the others. It's because I believe in you. As much as I have loathed you, I love you. And, even though I tried to leave you, I love you. I hate you, yet you're my best friend. You are my friend, my lover, my mistress, I will always be the one who will endure the pain, and because I love you...Many know you. Many others have loved you...Some have even called you bad names, far worse than a slut or whore, they called you sports entertainment, but not me. I called you my love, and I called you by your name, Professional Wrestling! I love you my mistress, you continue to pull me back into you. I am that kid who watches and believes, I am a fan, I am one the boys, I am your man, I am you, and you are me, Pro Wrestling, my lust, my desire, my love, my mistress, no matter how bad my body hurts and my heart breaks, I still love you my mistress! PRO WRESTLING!

# ✣ 50 Shades of Blaze ✣

*Sometimes reality is the strangest fantasy of all.*

I was married once, just once. Once was enough for me. Just like I dated a girl from Alabama once, just once. Hell, I waited until I was thirty to get married for the first time, and now at fifty, if I could go back and do it again, I'd wait another thirty. There's always that old saying about never saying never, well, rest assured, this is one area of my life that I can say never. I hope I didn't curse myself into another marriage with that last line. Well, if I did, I hope my next wife, is rich and owns a liquor store. You know what they say, "First time love, and second time money."

Anyway, this isn't going to be some sleazy, kinky, twisted kind of story where I drop the names of some or a few, or even a couple of the girls, or ladies, if you can call them that that I've "dated". I really just thought it would be a way to illustrate to you how when you're young, maybe have a few dollars in your bank account, and out on the wrestling circuit or living that lifestyle how easy it is to get laid. Isn't that a good enough reason to get into the wrestling business in the first place, to get laid? That's kind of my point here, when you're young and single that's the easy fun part, especially for a wrestler. Then when you get a little older and settle down some, have a wife, a couple of kids and a home, that perspective changes. Now, in my situation, as mentioned I was married but that changed after several years for whatever reason, and for reasons I won't go into in this book. Now don't be too quick to judge. Things happen as life throws you a little twist every now and again, so you learn to live with it and move on. Life isn't always, sunshine, rainbows and lollipops. I can say this; it wasn't for a lack of love or trying on my behalf. I place no blame on anyone. Life happens! In my situation, getting a divorce was actually a blessing in disguise. Women, I love them, but I know how treacherous, cunning, and twisted some of these bitches can be. That's why I say once was enough for me. I'm happier and better off single. If you don't believe me, just look around at people in unhappy marriages. Look at the people you know that are divorced, broke, who wished they could get out of their marriage. That goes for both men and

3

women. So, for me, onward and upward we go as that situation ended and I was back to being single again.

So you go from being single, to having a wife, and back to being single. Now what? Being in wrestling, and being a wrestler, but now being a little older and maybe somewhat wiser the train of thought changes once again. And the thought is this: the thought of all that free pussy seems forever elusive. But as you will see it's never free, smarten up, because you always pay the rent one way or another. Trust me on that. In my case when you're not out on the road where, after the show ends, there's girls waiting, young, pretty, and many wanting sex and nothing else, they're now gone. You feel like your life has become boring and all that easy sex is gone forever. But, it's not! Now, again, don't be so fast to judge, there's girls out there who are just as willing, but since you're no longer in the spotlight, so to say, night after night, you just have to pay.

Marriage is the final sale, and I'm not in the market for any final sales! But with strippers and escorts you are only renting. To me, it's better than owning if you think about it. I don't judge how one makes a living, and to me, I just look at it like another service. It's just like all other services. It's a service like having new carpet installed in your home, getting the engine on your car fixed, or having the plumber come over to unclog the shit that's stopping up your toilet; you pay that person for the services rendered. It's the same thing.

Marlon Brando said it best in the movie, *Burn*. Of course, take into consideration he was speaking only on an economic level. "Now, a wife must be provided with a home, with food, with dresses, with medical attention, etc., etc. You're obligated to keep her a whole lifetime even when she's grown old and perhaps a trifle unproductive. And then, of course, if you have the bad luck to survive her, you have to pay for the funeral. Now with a prostitute, on the other hand, it's quite a different matter, isn't it? You see, there's no need to lodge her or feed her, certainly no need to dress her or to bury her, thank God. She's yours only when you need her, you pay her only for that service, and you pay her by the hour!"

I've said before, "You always have to pay the rent, one way or another," so I'll stick to the pay as you go service and

4

be all the happier. With that said, not all "dates" or girls have been paid services, at least not by the hour. I've met some pretty cool chicks in my time, prior to marriage, um, friends only when married, and a bunch of fun dates now that girls aren't exactly lining up outside the dressing room door waiting to be escorted to a cheap hotel for the night.

Now, again, I'm not going to drop names or brag about babes I've bagged, but I'll be more than glad to share some funny stories about "dates" I've had. Sometimes reality is the strangest fantasy of all. I refer a lot of these times to as, "Bobby Blaze Entertainment" so I'll share a few with you.

The first story that comes to mind happened on a blind date. I had been talking to this girl on the phone for a couple of weeks when we decided to meet in a public place. I was thinking of a normal evening date when she suggested that we meet in a local supermarket parking lot because it would be easier to find her there than, "Where she was staying." I found this strange, but when she said that morning hours worked best for her I became even more leery of this "date." So, on a weekday morning at ten o'clock I was heading to meet this little darling of a girl when my phone rings and it's her, "Hey can you meet me down the street from the store, I'm walking that way now and it's starting to rain." I agree and keep going, "past the store, up over a little hill and around that curve, and you'll see me walking your way" I heard as I remained on the phone with her. I wasn't about to let this little honey get away from me. I was going on a date and maybe find the love of my life. So, through the light mist of a spring rain, there she is, standing on a street corner in a green knit sweater, baggie green sweat pants tucked into brown Uggs. Yep, that's my girl. I pick her up and ask where she would like to go and she says that McDonald's would be nice. Once inside they are still serving breakfast, unlike now when it's served all day, every day. Anyway, I order a Coke and tell her to get whatever she wants. This is going to be one expensive date I can already tell as she orders two, not one, but two ninety-nine cent sausage biscuits and a large Coke as well.

We proceed to our table and as soon as I am seated she has already torn into one of the biscuits. She's already unwrapping the other one before I have the first sip of my

5

drink. Man, this is sad I begin thinking to myself. This poor girl hasn't eaten in days I bet. The thought of getting laid had long left my mind when she first got into the car. Being with this girl was the farthest thing from my mind. Although, I did think to myself, and only for a fleeting moment, "If this girl wants to give me some head it's most certain that I'll be using a condom because there's no way I'm letting her grungy yellowish green teeth near my manhood." Hey, I'm a guy, and it was only for a quick moment. I really felt sorry for her at this point as she finished eating and looked up from her tray and asked me if I was going to eat. I told her no but she was welcome to go get something else if she wanted. She didn't order more food but did go refill her drink.

When she sat back down and as we talked, I point blank asked her very seriously, "Do you do drugs?" Quicker than a rattle snake strike, she perked up and said, "Why, you got some?" I laughed out loud right in her face. I told her I didn't and wasn't interested in getting any or doing any with her either. She told me how crack scared her because she'd done it once, but not only that it kept her up all night. "I got into a threesome with my boyfriend and another girl and I don't even like girls." I ended up buying her a pack of cigarettes and dropping her off at the grocery store. So much for Bobby Blaze Entertainment, watching a meth head who hadn't eaten in God knows how long was very depressing.

I've been single for more years than I was married, and I've enjoyed being single a lot more. That's true even when dating someone. I keep searching for these little bits of free pussy and entertainment I guess because that's just the way I'm wired. Sure, paid services are fine, but I'm really more into the amusing hookups. And, girls, I'll never figure you all out anyway, so I may as well be amused. Ask any guy, when you have a girlfriend there's always a steady and ready supply of girls willing to hook up with you. But, the moment you don't have a girlfriend, you couldn't get laid in a morgue. You all know the feeling. It's like falling into a barrel full of nipples and come up sucking your thumb at times.

Another "date" I recall was almost as fun as the one with my little meth head. Almost being the key word here. I met this chick, actually two chicks after a show I attended one night, and the older of the two asked me for a ride home. After a few minutes of small talk and her convincing me that her house was just around the corner, I gave them a ride home being the fine Southern gentleman that I am. I also made a mental note as to which street and house I had dropped them off at. It really wasn't that far from the building and again after some small talk we exchanged numbers and agreed to meet again. A few days pass and I say to myself, "Ya know, that town wasn't that far away the other night, I think I'll drive back up there and see about getting lucky." So, I head back to where I had let them off just a few nights before. Sure enough she comes to the door. Now, she wasn't as pretty in the early morning light as she had been in the dimly lit building and parking lot a couple nights back, but she didn't look half bad. She tells me the other girl is still in bed but she'll get her up in a little bit. I find out she's in her late thirties and her friend is in her early twenties. Notice I'm not using names here and that reason isn't to protect the not innocent but rather because I never did find out their names. I referred to them as Sue Bob and Baby Girl. Sue Bob told me she had been a stripper for a couple of years and she was going to help the younger of the two get into the business of stripping and escorting.

She told me she was willing to do anything to start making some money again and wanted to know if I could help her meet some men. I gathered she wanted me to pimp her out as she was going to teach the younger girl the game and pimp her out. Hell, I don't know to this day. I just knew something wasn't right about this little sexual adventure. A little time passes when Baby Girl comes into the room wearing only panties and a smile. Now, I like that, but I still get a sense that something just isn't right. Sue Bob explains to me that they are down on their luck and wouldn't mind a little donation for their time and services. Let me again be clear on this matter, I have no problem making donations especially if I think I'm getting a two for the price of one deal. But, before anything can happen Sue Bob says, "I need you to run me out to get a pack of smokes and over by the food bank so I can pick up our food for the week." Okay, talk about your down on your luck ex-strippers and future escorts, I think I've just hit rock bottom. By the way, did I mention this was in West Virginia? Anyway, here's one girl, "Baby Girl" sitting topless, the other, "Sue Bob" asking for some smokes and a ride to the food bank, then it's, "We'll do anything you want." And away we go.

Baby Girl stays there while I go through a tobacco drive-thru with Sue Bob and over to the local food bank. So, here it is, almost noon, and I'm sitting on a public street with some ex-stripper chick that just walked half-assed naked into the community food pantry. I didn't know if they were giving out soup or salad or super pussy, so I stayed in the car.

I don't know if I expected one of the boys to jump out of nowhere with a video camera to say I had been punked or if the cops were going to pull up behind me and tell me to, "Calmly step out of the car sir." The longer I sat there the more paranoid I became. I was thinking this is one weird situation to be in all over the possibility of getting a piece of ass or two. And, just like that, I kicked out on two as if someone set a match under my ass. I started my car and drove the hell out of there. I ran a stop sign, two red lights, took a left across moving traffic, didn't yield, headed west on I-64 and didn't slow down until I hit the first exit in Kentucky.

For the record, besides the episodes like those just mentioned, I have met and dated some really cool girls along the way. Many have been friends for years and I have nothing bad to say about any of them. Those that have gotten to know me through the years will probably say the same thing about me. They all get the same speech from date number one. "I'm not gonna be your next husband and I don't want any more kids." That's just me. I'm a better friend than I am a boyfriend and that's all cool and the gang with me. So now I think you may get my drift when I say it's just a lot easier for me to make a donation than it is to find someone to settle down with or God forbid, marry. So, to all the women in the world I've loved before, thank you. And, as for you dear reader get your mind out of the gutter, I don't kiss and tell, that's all the fifty shades of Blaze you'll be getting from me...at least for now.

Wait a minute here. Backup! I'm getting ahead of myself. By now you're probably wondering what this has to do with professional wrestling. Well we'll get to that here shortly; this is just a small example of the kind of things I get into throughout this book. It's just another illustration of me being able to kick out on two and all a part of my wrestlers' education, and as you will see, one thing just led to another.

## ⊰ Train Ride ⊱

*"You wanna be a wrestlin' star?" "No I just wanna be a wrestler." From about 1983 through 1985 with StarrCade and the first WrestleMania coming up in a few short months, my answer wasn't yeah, it was, "FUCK YEAH!"*

There's a letter from a journal I kept in 1983 which is included in, *Pin Me Pay Me, Have Boots Will Travel* as proof to the fact about me really wanting to break into pro wrestling one day. At the time, I wasn't quite sure how, but I did have a good idea that I would be involved in the professional wrestling industry at some point in my life.

My first exposure to professional wrestling that I can recall was that of the old WWWF back in around 1968 or so before moving from Baltimore, Maryland to Ashland, Kentucky. I had only seen it on a television at my grandmother's house. I do remember enjoying it an awful lot. After that, the next time I watched wrestling on TV was when my younger brother excitedly called me inside the house one Saturday afternoon to show me something on the TV, it was wrestling. It was the old Memphis wrestling that I was ultimately brought up on.

I was hooked from that day on. I eventually started to go to pro wrestling shows, and did so for years as a kid. I used to go to the old ICW shows that would come through monthly during my younger years. I had been to the other local indie shows as well as the Memphis wrestling show that would come through Ashland a couple times a year. Also during this time, 1983–1984, I went to several NWA and WWF shows in Lexington, Kentucky as well as in Huntington and Charleston, West Virginia. I just knew I was going to break in as soon as I got some professional training. It didn't happen immediately, but it did happen.

I knew it had to be a business, from a couple of prior conversations with a couple of the wrestlers that I had spoken to around this time period. But, by the same token, I knew where to draw the line. I wasn't going to insult or disrespect professional wrestling or any of the wrestlers when I spoke to them. I sure as hell didn't want, Dr. D David Schultz busting my ear drum if I ever ran into him. Keep in mind, the wrestling business was still kayfabed then. But, also keep in mind that with the upcoming first ever WrestleMania pay–per–view coming up, there was a lot of media hype. Professional wrestling was just about to become more main stream than ever, and the entire business was about to change forever.

On March 15, 1985, I was on a train from Baltimore, Maryland to Ashland, Kentucky. Yes, I was once again living in Baltimore and had been for several months at this time. I was now getting exposed to watching a lot of WWF on television. At this point, keep in mind that I had only seen the WWF back as a young kid and only once again during a summer I had spent there in 1979. Back then without the internet, my only connection with the stars of the WWF was through all the magazines my brother and I used to buy, or sometimes trade through snail mail with my uncle who lived in Baltimore. Each month when we bought these magazines we would put a check mark by who we had seen wrestle on TV in each of the "official rankings" from each territory. We would put a circle around a guy's name if we had seen him in person. My brother, my uncle, and I did this for years. On the rare occasion of a phone conversation or visits, we would compare who we had seen or who we thought were the best and usually end up trading magazines or show programs that we also collected.

During that winter of 1985, I actually got to see the WWF on a weekly basis and could see that there was a big difference between what I had been watching for years, Memphis wrestling and what they were doing on their TV. To me it wasn't that they had the bigger stars because keep in mind I had now also been exposed to the NWA, and to me, those guys were the real deal, and the better wrestlers. But, I could see that the wrestlers and the programming were so much bigger and that the guys there seemed to be pushed as real superstars. I had heard about and seen places like Madison Square Garden, The Spectrum, and The Boston

Garden on television because I was such a basketball fan as well, but to actually see, when the WWF ran shows there and the places were sold out for professional wrestling and maybe that week's program showed footage from those places it was unreal.

I could just tell that there was something different when watching the WWF, as opposed to watching my wrestling from Memphis, and even different from watching the NWA. I was still able to watch the NWA shows that were being aired too, but again there was a difference. You have to remember I was basically raised on Memphis wrestling and, sure, on some Saturday mornings, "Live from the ring," when Lance Russell, alongside of Dave Brown, "And boy do we have a big day of championship wrestling for you," might show something big from the sold out Mid-South Coliseum, where they, "Did things right on a Monday night," but you could just tell that the WWF was just in a league of its own. Again, keep in mind this is all around the time that VKM was expanding and there were guys who had been stars in other areas of the country now working in the WWF, so it made these guys who I had seen, who were stars on these smaller shows, now look like even bigger stars. Man, that's when pro wrestling was still fun. Don't get me wrong, it's still fun, but it's just different. Little did we all know how all that was about to change with this big pay-per-view event known as WrestleMania coming up on March 31st of that year and with the internet in the not too distant future.

I also got to go watch two house shows at The Baltimore Arena while I was there. One was an NWA show and was just as awesome as the ones I had seen back in Huntington and Charleston. The other was my first live WWF show. These two shows were held within a month of each other, like one was in January and the other was in February, and both of the shows had packed houses. A couple of things stand out in my mind. One was that Sgt. Slaughter wrestled on both shows. I had to look it up, but this was around the time he was in a dispute over some kind of action figure deal he had and some deal the WWF had on action figures. I think he even worked for the AWA during that year as well. Either way, he worked both of the shows that I saw. I also had only seen Jimmy "Superfly" Snuka on TV and wanted to see him

11

in person and get as close as possible to see how big he was. I remember standing down by the back door when not only Snuka walked in, but right beside him was Tony Atlas. It was like they were bigger than I had imagined as they both had on these big white parka jackets, and they were huge. I couldn't believe how gigantic they both looked as they walked into the arena that night. Of course they looked just as impressive once in the ring with bodies like they had. Even though I had seen guys in the NWA with great bodies, these guys were not only big, they were chiseled.

So now that, I've gone around the world to cross the street, I'll finish my train ride story. On that train ride home, I met a young guy close to my age. We started talking about wrestling and I guess we talked wrestling for 8-10 hours of the 12 hour ride. We talked about the upcoming HUGE pay-per-view, how to get into the business, our favorite matches and wrestlers and favorite moments. I told him that I was going to be a wrestler one day and he said he was going to as well. I never saw this guy after that March 15th train ride and often wonder if he ever tried to become a professional wrestler or even attempted to do so.

If you've read my other book then you know how much training I went through. I knew from an early age that I wanted to be a pro wrestler, and I knew when I was talking to this guy, I had my mind made up and I was serious about breaking in. It took time, dedication, and I made sacrifices that maybe this guy was never willing to make. Maybe you're a wrestler who is reading this right now, and recall talking to a long haired young man on a train ride, and you remember me. Maybe you went on to super stardom in wrestling, or maybe you just went back to wherever you were going that day, and settled into a nice comfortable life after you finished school or college, I don't know. What I do know is, whoever you are, wherever you are, I know I told you on that long train ride that I was going to be a professional wrestler one day, and by God, I did. Of all the many long train rides I had ever been on prior to this one between Ashland and Baltimore, and the many more that I would be on in countries like Australia and Japan, this was the one I'll never forget. I was just a young enthusiastic fan dying for a chance to one day break into professional wrestling, and I eventually did.

## ∾ So You Wanna Be A Wrestler ∾

So you wanna be a wrestler? Well, I wasn't able to just step off that train ride I was telling you about and break into wrestling. I wish I could tell you it was that simple but that wasn't and isn't the case. I had to come up with a plan. It took a couple of years, but my plan worked. Maybe, if you take some of the advice I leave you here in this book, and learn from some of my mistakes, you will make it into the exciting, lucrative world of professional wrestling, otherwise, "Welcome to the wonderful world of minimum wages baby." It's my honest opinion that before you start trying to make wrestling a priority nowadays, you should start with a Plan B. I recently had a talk to Jim Cornette about having a Plan B. He was telling me back when he was first getting involved in wrestling you didn't need a Plan B because you could actually make money and make a decent living from having so many bookings and towns to make each week. "Professional wrestling was your plan; you didn't need a Plan B." I wanted wrestling to be my Plan A, but I also took a lot of odd jobs and did many different things to make extra money once I decided it was time to finally make up my mind that, "Now is the time I make my run and break into wrestling." I didn't have a Plan B either, at least not at this point in my life, because all I knew was, "I want to wrestle." So, first things first, have a Plan B. Make sure you have something to fall back on if things don't work out in the wrestling business the way you want them to.

Make wrestling your top priory, or your number one goal, but do so with a backup plan. I've said it before and I've explained it before, "Go get trained, professionally!" Go to the gym, work out, train, listen, learn, and work hard during your training. While you're working a "real" job or as some of these young guys nowadays say, "A shoot job," it's important to keep training, keep learning, and keep taking matches any and everywhere you can get booked. But, keep in mind, you don't know everything, and I say that no matter how many matches you have had even after getting the proper training. Don't give up your day job.

No matter what, when you do go to a town or are booked somewhere, whether you have a horrible job or a great job, whether you think wrestling is your Plan A, or are smart enough to have a Plan B, no matter what the situation or circumstances, always, and I mean always present yourself professionally.

Once you have trained, again with a respectable trainer or well-known professional then make sure you have a resume, just like you would in a real world job. You are trying to sell yourself. You may even consider yourself a whore at this point. If you're not, don't worry; in time this business will make you a whore. That's why you have the Plan B, being a whore isn't for everyone. As I've mentioned before, "You work the business, don't let the business work you." In other words, don't let the business use you up, because it will. Learn to make the most of it and work it to your advantage. So, let's get back to the resume. You should have your real name, your work or ring name, along with your stats, height, weight, etc. on it. Make sure you have your up to date contact information on it, even if you're living in a car, have a contact number. Include pictures, not the ones Aunt Flo took of you out behind your house or the ones your mommy took of you if you're still living in her basement. Get a professional photographer and have professional photos of yourself. List your trainers name and contact information if possible. Write out some of the experience that you have and make a short list of companies that you have worked for. Don't list the little backyard shows that you got booked on or booked yourself when you ran little neighborhood shows thinking you're a rassler. List a couple, and you should have at least a couple of shows that you actually worked that had names. I realize you probably won't be listing the WWE or any other big name company, but think big, and if you worked for a reputable company, then make sure you list it. Real experience! No amount of ink on a page can cover the fact that you're a shitty wrestler if you haven't been trained properly and have little experience. Go so far as to list your real life marketable abilities and skills. Lastly, list or use references. Just like in your Plan B or real job, make sure you list people who you know, and people who know your name as soon as it's mentioned.

Now you want bookings? That's simple. Be present! That's right, go to every show you can go to whether you're booked or not, show up, help sell tickets, set up the ring, clean up the dressing room, set up chairs, do something, but whatever you do, don't be at home in mommy's basement playing on that fucking X-Box, drinking Mountain Dew, wishing you were booked somewhere tonight when you know that there are shows going on somewhere in your area. It could be a big company like WWE, TNA, ROH, or a small local show, but the worst and most you'll be out is a little gas money, and the price of a ticket, but be there. If there's a ring set up, you be there, and once you're present, if it's a big show and you're not booked, sit down, shut up, watch and learn. If it's a small local indie show then do as I said, do something to help out. Be present!

Once you're present, don't make this a onetime appearance by just giving them your resume, and then never come back. Persistence! You have to be persistent. I called, talked, and went to several WCW shows before I actually signed my contract. I was persistent in my contacts with Jim

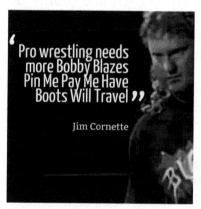

' Pro wrestling needs more Bobby Blazes Pin Me Pay Me Have Boots Will Travel ''

Jim Cornette

Cornette and people at SMW, nine months of contact to be exact before I even got a tryout match. Show up at every show and again, do whatever you have to do. Help set up that ring every month, sell those tickets, help with the music, do something, but be present and be persistent. Yes, I'm being redundant. That's so maybe this will start to sink in a little bit. Be persistent!

The next thing you have to do is have patience. This may be the hardest part, but you just have to be patient. If you're professional, present, and persistent, be patient and it will pay off. So, here's your quick review to satisfy my OCD and hopefully help you get your ass booked somewhere one day: Be Professional! Be Present! Be Persistent! Be Patient!

## ᕲ Two ᕲ

*"Is there anyone so wise as to learn by the experience of others?"—Voltaire*

## ᕲ Listen Up ᕲ

I've often heard it said from several other veterans in the wrestling business that "What's new is old, and what's old is new." With that being said, so many of these young guys today don't even take the time to listen to a well-respected ring vet. Even after I had trained and gone full time into the wrestling business, I couldn't begin to tell you how many times I went back and sought out Dean Malenko to get his opinion on something that I did in the ring. I sought him out the night I signed my contract with World Championship Wrestling to see what he thought of it and if it was fair. I still listen and take in what I'm being told by guys that I've known or been around for twenty-five years. I worked for Jim Cornette for three years, how could I not learn something from listening to him? I still listen to Bobby Fulton whenever I'm around him or talking to him on the phone. Why wouldn't I take the time to listen to men like them? So what's one thing that's missing in professional wrestling? One thing is guys are not taking the time to listen. Listening is missing! The guys I see in locker rooms and out in the ring today don't listen; they talk about every spot they are going to be doing in their match. So, in turn when I watch their match, they go to the ring and don't know how to listen to the fans. They've already called everything in the back and have that, "I've got to get my shit in mentality." Whatever happened to having a good idea about a spot or two if it's there, knowing the finish, and then going out there, listening to the fans reacting to your actions in the ring, and when the time is right, hit the finish? It's that simple. Get the people involved by interacting with them through your actions in the ring. Make it real, make it believable and they will come back again.

I've often said people don't want to go to a wrestling show to see themselves. They want to see someone bigger than life. They want to see guys with good bodies, guys that can wrestle, guys that have something special, a character if you will. They need to see something that they don't see every day in their office or out on their real jobs every day. They want to escape, so, no one wants to see themselves, they want to believe, and it's us, the performers who have to give them something to believe in, make them live in that or those moments of suspended belief of reality.

I tell guys all the time, "Think shoot, and then work." Let the people know that we're here to fight not put a show on. The suspension of disbelief. Make them want to believe, because they want to believe. Hell, everyone knows it's a show, but don't give it away by just going through the motions.

Give them a damn fight. Have a reason to be having a match in the first place. Once you're involved in the match, give them a wrestling match, not a ten minute high spot fest. Wrestle, work, do a spot, give the fans a place or a spot where they can clap, cheer, boo, then repeat. If it's a ten minute high spot when are the fans going to have a time to clap?

Oh sure you got your stuff in, but many of the fans were over buying popcorn because you didn't give them a reason to watch. Worst is if they did sit there and start watching you, then you lost them because they were seeing a dance contest, not a wrestling match. If you're doing your job in the ring, they will watch, get involved, and as I said, repeat until the fans are at their highest point of excitement, then it's time to take it home or go into the finish and everyone wins because when you hear that big pop at the finish, you'll know it was worth listening to the fans, and the fans will appreciate your match. Listen up!

## ◈ Speaketh Not To Fools For They Despise Knowledge ◈

When given the opportunity I really like to help younger or less experienced wrestlers by giving them advice. So many people helped me along the way; I think I'm somewhat obligated to pass on some of my knowledge to others. I got to live my dream and it gives me great pleasure in seeing some young talent get out there make it in the world of wrestling. I think it's important to encourage the other talent out there. I had my time. The younger guys and girls coming up are the future of the industry. Even though at times I may come across as being harsh or it may seem like I'm being a hard ass at times, I do try to encourage them. Like many businesses the wrestling business is tough to succeed in, so if I take the time to critique a match or an entire show, I am at least honest about it. It's also because I want to make them work harder or maybe it will give them a boost to see them far exceed anything they have thought they could do with the business.

One of the problems I have though, and it really just depends on where that person is in their career, is when it comes to being paid. The business I have the most experience in is obviously professional wrestling. Now I know everyone has to start somewhere, so not everyone is just going to go out and make a ton of money right out of the gate. But, it's called professional wrestling, and professionals get paid. They get paid for their talent, creative ideas, experience, and for, with all things being equal, which I realize they aren't, but they get paid for working on the show.

Are you really a professional if you're not being paid? Doing a show once every other month or so, usually less than forty miles from your home, does not classify nor qualify you as a professional wrestler. I realize many would trade in their soul for a chance at the big time.

I've been to the top, traveled to many countries outside of the United States, worked for more independent promotions than I can count and at one point worked for two of the biggest professional wrestling companies in the world. My question is why do so many ask me questions when they aren't ready for my answers? I'm sure there are many other guys out there who have probably tried to help some of these goofs as well, and have found it just as frustrating. As many times as I've had someone take my advice, and it's not because I know it all, but they were sincere in their questions about their career, more often than not, when they took the advice I gave them, it proved to be right. But, for that one who listens to what I tell him, there's another twenty who ask or seek my advice, but once I give it to them, it's useless to them because they already know it all. That person, "the know it all," the one working—wrestling for free even, thinks they already know it all. That is amazing to me. Why the hell did they even ask my opinion if they already know it all? They are the fools of which I speak. You're really not worthy of my time even though I tried to help you in some way. You just never got it. You never will!

There are many who I've have helped, and I'm sure that if you're one who I did help, you have now met many of the fools for which I speak. I take great pride in the fact that it gives me pleasure to play a small part in helping someone else or seeing them succeed or become better as a performer. Thanks for listening. My request for these so called, "smarks," or "rasslers" is to please stop. By the way, that's an oxymoron, you're either smart to the business or you're not. You're a fan, or you're a mark for the business, but you can't be a smart mark.

Stop killing the business! Stop killing the business you claim to love. If you love it, you will quit it, buy a ticket like the fan you claim to be, and go back to school or get a real job that actually does pay. That's a hard truth! There, I just gave you a nickels worth of truth and advice for free. That's five cents more then you will make trying to work on these little indie shows, so take it.

Here are the ones who need to take this advice to heart: Guys who run spots where it looks like two meth heads on roller blades. Spot monkeys! Get the fuck out of the ring! Guys who are five foot nothing and weigh less than a buck fifty soaking wet. Get the fuck into the gym! Wait, I think I had something else to mention to you, yeah, I did. Get the fuck out of the ring! And last but not least, fools. The very fools, to whom I dedicate this particular story, get the fuck out of our business! Now, guess how many fucks the fans give about you or your shitty match? Zero! I'll be more kind. I'll give two shits and a fuck...Now, GET THE FUCK OUT OF THE RING!!!

# ✎ Getting an Education ✎

## *Road and Ring Education*

Now that you have a little better understanding of working for money and being happy, how about a couple of stories about working the indies? Eddie Watts used to say, "Every meals a banquet, everyday a holiday, a life better than the president." That's when I was making about five hundred Canadian dollars per week which converted to about $67.50 per day in US dollars. I'm sure he heard it somewhere else when he was first breaking into the business. But, I was getting my education as a wrestler as I was kicking out on two every night and winning most of my matches. Right there's another good reason to work the indies, you get to go over, ha–ha, again, I kid. But seriously, if you're booked in a program, booking the show, or are being used strong on a show, especially in a territory, you have to stay strong, and you have to kick out on two. Lesson learned? Save your money! The real mark is the one in the ring making $67.50 per night, not the one paying $8.00 for a folding chair in the front row for the show that night.

On one of my first shows, way back in 1988, when many people still believed in wrestling, as in when it was still considered a competitive sport, I earned another lesson. When there's a little old man sitting in the front row at a show, or even a little old lady with an umbrella, watch your back. Once in Virginia, this little old man went to grab my shirt and jacket as I set it down in the corner. I watched him slowly get out of his seat and while using a cane, he slowly tried to make his way to the ring to "steal" my stuff. Well, I grabbed my shirt without knowing it had gotten tangled and caught the loop of his cane. I gave a swift jerk and he just about took a bump right there against the ring or on the floor by the ring post. Luckily the baby face caught him just in time, hit me, threw me back into the ring and we had our match. Needless to say, it did get me over pretty easy as a heel that night. Lesson learned? Watch out for old people in the front row at shows!

It's not all glitz and glamor. Many nights on the road you're not out in front of a sold out show. There are many long rides night after night wrestling in high school gyms,

20

recreation centers, and armories. That's just all a part of being in the business. I had a big paid show lined up for a county fair once and took an indie booking the night before which was a fund raiser. I thought it would be a good idea for myself and my opponent to use this one as a tune up match for the bigger show while maybe making a dime and having some fun.

The fund raiser, bless their heart was for a food bank. The admission for the show was two cans of canned goods or other non-perishable items. Four people showed up! The ring was up, my opponent, "The Masked Scorpion," and I both declined the ten dollars offered to us to perform. What we did was, we asked the promoter if we could just go on first and have our match. This was in a sweltering old gymnasium and since we both were in shape and had already been training for bigger and better things to come; we knew they needed the money more than we did. Besides, we were working on the big paid show the following evening. Plus, I was already booked and would soon be heading off to Canada for a sixteen week tour. The ten dollars meant nothing, but the experience meant everything, plus four people had shown up expecting to see wrestling. We did our match, thanked the guys running the show, shook everyone's hands and headed back home. It was only about thirty minutes away, so it really was worth it for us as it did provide us with a good workout, and made us feel good knowing that the four fans did get to see a good match. The next night, over 600 people showed up to see a really good free professional wrestling show at the local county fair. So one night you're in front of four people, the next night it's 600. Both nights, the fans, at least during my and Scorpion's bout, got to see a highly competitive pro wrestling match. Lesson learned? You work just as hard in front of a small crowd of fans as you do in front of a large crowd. The fans deserve it!

Never stop learning, because life never stops teaching. Anyway, these are just a few of the stories and lessons that I learned out on the road and through wrestling. Just like I made mention of in, *Pin Me Pay Me*, I'm a lifelong, life time learner. I only mentioned a couple of stories because they are being used as a tie-in to my education story a little later in the book. Always be willing to learn. There are lessons, sometimes that you are unaware of in just about everything around you, from the people you meet to the places you've been. And, even though I'm going to give you a little look into my formal educational background, guess what? Everything I needed to know, I learned from being a professional wrestler.

Reading, writing, geography, math, science, social studies, English and other languages were all picked up and expanded upon from being around the wrestling business. Don't get me wrong, I'm proud of my formal education, and from my old neighborhood and junior high school I was able to pick up a few street smarts along the way, but pro wrestling taught me more about myself and about life than I ever learned in school or from a book.

Reading as you will soon find out didn't always come so easy for me, but I had to learn. I learned to read everything from programs to line-ups. I learned to read posters, travel arrangements, booking sheets, and itineraries. Being able to read, saved my butt on many occasions. I am thankful that I learned how to read.

Writing, well, I had to learn how to write everything from signing my name to checks to signing autographs. I learned to write wrestling stories for event programs, to press releases, to the books that I write today. Even though I have a degree in communications, most of what I write comes from the heart and through being able to write it all down, speaks well for my English, or at times, lack thereof as I sometimes drop in a bunch of GD's, F-Bombs, and other choice words, but I can get my point across nonetheless.

Geography, hey, GPS systems were just coming out when I was on my way out of the business. I had to learn how to read a map. In addition to reading that map, and having seen a globe or two in my day, I could actually see and know where or what part of the country or world I was actually wrestling in.

That's all pretty neat stuff to me. I've been on five of the seven continents. I've personally seen rivers, oceans and seas that others have only read about. I've swum in The Gulf Of Mexico, The Atlantic and Pacific Oceans as well as The

Indian Ocean. Again, just pretty neat stuff, because I'm not that good of a swimmer, but I've been in them.

On social studies or civics, I've been a goodwill ambassador for the United States of America as I have visited these other countries and actually met people and have gotten to know what is going on in the world and I've learned the world isn't flat and doesn't end out at the city limits of Ashland, Kentucky. Along with English, I have picked up a few words and sentences in Spanish and Japanese. One also learns more about social causes and how different parts of the world think as opposed to how we are taught to think in America.

Now I can only do simple math, adding, subtraction, multiplication, and division, as I never got much into algebra or past the basics, but these basics were all I needed to know out on the road. You either make money or you lose money. If you are hungry and need to eat, you look into your wallet, pocket, or fanny pack and buy and pay for whatever you can afford for that meal. The same can be said for living expenses, hotels, rental cars, etc. The car you buy or the house you own, well those things cost money, so you work, make money, and you buy them. The more you make, the better the options are or the more the possibilities open up as to what you can afford. That's simple math and basic economics 101 right there.

So, anyway, there's your basic education in a nut shell from the education of a wrestler. KISS, "Keep It Simple Stupid" comes to mind. Just pay attention to what's required or what's going on around you. Do your job. Work hard at your job, and try to always do the right things and most of the time everything will work itself out the way it's supposed to. "The only thing more expensive than education is ignorance," as Ben Franklin said.

## ⌇ Tips for Indie Guys ⌇

• If you wear a hood, known as a "mask" for the casual fan, learn how to work in it. If you're wearing a hood and playing weekend warrior in the ring, listen. The fans can't see your eyes and facial expressions; use your hands, arms, and overall body language. Work your gimmick!

- If you have a replica belt and wrestle in front of 42 people once a month that does not make you a professional wrestler. Having the replica belt sure as hell doesn't make you a champion either.
- Just because you can do a back flip off the top rope does not make you a pro wrestler.
- You fucking indie brats who give away the finish by the way you walk or the way you mope when going to the ring when you're going lose. Why? Get excited! It takes talent to get someone else over. Grow up you mark! Better yet, buy a ticket!
- Wrestling is all about the sell. A good way to practice this is to practice your facial sells and body language in front of a mirror. This is also the best way to learn how to cut a promo—stare yourself down during it, see yourself as the fan would and figure out how to make that eye contact to create a connection.
- The more often you let people kick out of your finisher the less valuable of a move it becomes.
- I'm begging you to stop with the false finishes that the stars on TV use in all of your matches as real finishes. You're not Superman! If the major star uses something as a finish, don't use it as a false finish in your match. Show some respect!
- Finally, treat the business with respect. Get proper training from a top trainer and learn to be a good wrestler and eventually, a good worker. I just do not understand how someone can, with all of today's training facilities, wrestling schools, especially with the WWE having an all-out, "Performance Center" not get better or think they know it all. There are also guys like, "Hustler" Rip Rogers, offering one-on-one training, and other known and well respected guys like Dr. Tom Prichard, Les Thatcher, and Al Snow who have, "been there and done that" doing seminars. Go to one of their seminars! Why be so lazy or make up some lame excuse to not go and try to learn something or try to improve yourself? I just don't get it. And, please don't use the excuse that you think you know it all. You don't!

No wonder professional wrestling, especially on the indie scene is in the shape it's in. Train! Go to a seminar! Take private lessons! Do something! Don't be like the rest! Think outside the box! Smarten the fuck up! Lions do not lose sleep over the opinions of sheep. If you want to break into pro wrestling or learn the business, then learn it the right way. Train! One hour per day is not asking too much to give of yourself towards achieving your goal. Study or watch film/videos! Go to seminars when offered in your area! Again, smarten the fuck up! To borrow a line from Nike, "Just Do It!" That does not mean working for free once you have been trained. That means, if you have been trained, never give up, keep training, keep learning, and once you have the power to get booked, don't sell yourself short and work free, especially if that means traveling 500 miles to a show for free. What are you, a fan, a mark, or a trained professional?

• One final note, whether you're on the indie scene or you've made it to the top of the world of professional wrestling, always remember the number one rule for being on the road, and that is, "The number–one rule of the road is never go to bed with anyone crazier than yourself. You break this rule and you will be sorry." Kris Kristofferson

• Good Luck in your Future Endeavors!

RICKY MORTON, BOBBY BLAZE, & SABU vs. TOMMY RICH, TRACY SMOTHERS, & DOUG GILBERT

## ✒ Three ❧

*"The quality of any advice anybody has to offer has to be judged against the quality of life they actually lived."*
*Douglas Adams, The Ultimate Hitchhikers Guide*

## ✒ Let's Make Professional Wrestling a Sport Again ❧

Maybe, just maybe there's still time to bring pro wrestling back. I'm not talking about not having predetermined finishes or it ever returning to straight shoots, but what about having shows where winning and losing matters and counts? One of the things I see lacking on a lot of the shows I attend today is the fact that most of the younger guys are playing weekend wrestler and are only trying to emulate what they see on television, and sadly they are only seeing WWE TV. That is not a dig against the WWE. I personally enjoy NXT as well as the WWE using established stars who have been working years for other companies and in other countries. I've used a saying from the movie, *The Silence of the Lambs* for years, and that is, "We covet that which we see." These guys see these wrestling shows that are on TV, and that's all they know. Most are too damn cheap to buy a ticket to a house show and watch the guys who have made it to the WWE. Go! Do yourself a favor and go just to see how talented those guys and girls working there truly are. Oh, they all also go to the gym and look like professional athletes by the way.

If you're not on TV and still working on the indie scene you should always be trying to improve yourself and your look. If you have to explain yourself or the angle in a ten minute promo, you probably aren't getting over. The match in the ring should tell the story. That's what's important. These little story lines you see on TV are just that, story lines. It's not, or at least pro wrestling shouldn't be, about what happens outside the ring. You watch closely and you'll see what I'm talking about. Watch when a guy goes out of the ring there or after a match ends, and they cut away to a commercial, or something big happens up on the TitanTron and then that takes prevalence over the match. You're not in the WWE, you're not on TV. You are at a pro wrestling show or maybe an event, and there's a difference, but you can and need to tell the story in the ring and make professional wrestling a sport again. People will come. Of course, you have to have guys who can work, because the matches are what people are coming to see.

You don't have the power of television, and you're certainly not the WWE. Start your show or event with an actual wrestling match. Professional wrestling is what you advertised. You promoted live pro wrestling. Give them, the fans, professional wrestling. The fans will thank you.

Speaking of television and live events, if you have TV, even on a local or public access station, good for you, but please consider again you're not the WWE. Look at their production. Look at how much better the WWE produces their television. The production is so much better looking than that of TNA, and TNA's production is a better quality than that of ROH. There's just no comparison. I'm not talking talent, writers, story lines etc., I'm talking about the actual television production. Its top quality, it's like watching an NFL, MLB, NBA game or any number of reality shows when it comes to the production of the WWE.

When you have the kind of power that WWE and television brings with it, and that's all people see, or these new young guys watch or see, then it creates several problems for these wannabe promotions or wannabe wrestlers, again, most of whom are playing weekend warrior. Here are just three to name a few of these problems. 1) These numb nuts aren't getting trained properly. 2) They haven't been to a gym since 4th grade PE, and 3) they go out there and try to do what they only see on the television and it all just becomes make believe. I have a real problem with that. Make your match believable. TV or no TV, give the fans professional wrestling. As mentioned above, guys should know how to work, and those are the guys you put on your card, again, so the fans can enjoy a good match.

You can't have a shitty match and think you're great. You can't have a shitty body and expect people, especially true wrestling fans, to think you can actually win a match. Even with the power of television, you can't have a shitty match, get a win and have an announcer say, "What a spectacular match you've just witnessed wrestling fans." It doesn't work that way. Get a clue! Get the match over, have a good, great or that rare "spectacular" match, then whoever is doing commentary or announcing, whether it be televised or just at your local armory, they can actually say or tell it like it was. Have a professional announcer who is at least somewhat smart to the business. After the match is over, and it got over, the announcer can then tell the fans who won and can even add comments like, "What a great match you've just witnessed wrestling fans." That's the way it should be. It should be about who won, or how the baby face lost, and no matter who goes over, it's still a business, but at least there's the idea that it's still a sport, not a story or story line. Pro wrestling should be a sport!

## ◈ Leaders in the Locker Room ◈

Always listen to the fans when you're having a good match at an independent pro wrestling show. When it's time to take it home, then take it home. Getting that extra move in isn't going to matter. The "I gotta get my shit in" guy is killing his own match. You're killing the professional wrestling business. It was on life support, and you're out there trying to get your shit in, well hell, just pull the plug already, because you're killing it one extra, "gotta get it in there" move at a time. I've seen this several times on shows. Don't! There's a resurgence in indie professional wrestling, it's coming off the life support system, please, help keep the dream and the business alive. There will be other matches on other shows to get that move you so desperately had to try to get in. This won't be the case if you ruin a good match by doing it at the wrong time or when it isn't even necessary.

I've also discovered, and I don't think it's any great secret but I did find a huge problem on these indie shows. There's no one in the back holding the guys accountable for what guys do in the ring. Having a veteran, and I'm talking about a guy who actually knows how to run a locker room, would benefit these shows greatly. When a guy gets on the microphone when he shouldn't be on, that's a problem. Don't get on the microphone unless told to do so by the promoter or booker. Guys doing other guys moves that may already be planned out by a semi or main event match in your match takes away from the other matches. A heel who walks around with the fans after his match is just terrible for business. And you wonder why your company doesn't draw more fans. This isn't a dig or shot at any one organization as I've seen it happen on several indie shows. Why? It happens because no one is holding these idiots who probably shouldn't be booked anyway, accountable. If I ran the locker room or was the booker, these guys would be gone.

When a heel goes out and walks right by the baby face gimmick tables to get something to eat and then eats it with fans, well he is just an idiot. A heel shouldn't even come back out! Period! This is especially true if there's a hot finish in another match. Does anyone even know or remember what a hot match or a hot finish is anymore? I remember this happened to me twice and I smartened up quick about it. Once in Canada, a heel was involved in a match that involved a screw job finish and, as a heel there was no reason for me to be out there because if I saw my fellow friend or heel partner getting a decision reversed on him when he cheated, why wouldn't I go into the ring and attack the face? Thus I wasn't out there watching the match. I was hiding behind a side curtain where nobody could see me. I am not supposed to see that. The fans wouldn't think or believe in me very much if I had seen what was going on. So, I was smartened up in the back, "Don't go out or be seen during the main event tonight." That was when I was a heel. Now, switch gears or roles to when I was a baby face. In SMW working as a face I was walking back from the gimmick table and into the locker room. I watched the next match from behind the curtain. Right as the main event was about to start I was going to go out to get a soda pop or something to drink. Robert Gibson, said to me something along the lines of, "Hurry up and then be scarce Bobby, this match has a hot finish." I knew exactly what he meant. I couldn't be out there near the gimmick tables, the concession stands, or be in a place that I could be seen by the fans if I'm friends with the Rock-n-Roll Express and they are in a match that they will be getting screwed over in or cheated out of their belts in. Seriously, if they were my friends, as we are all friends and faces, and we were, if I'm watching, why wouldn't I or any other baby face run out there to help them or inform the ref as to what happened if we had seen it? It was a hot finish. There was no reason for me to see it. Again, see the above part where there's no one in the back to tell the guys these little things that can kill your match or kill your show. I appreciated Robert telling me this, and I appreciated it when the booker in Canada told me and smartened me up to a hot finish and why I shouldn't be out there and be seen by the fans. That's how one learns, someone, usually a veteran takes the time to help a young guy out about what to do during a show, during their match, and just how to conduct themselves in general in order to be a professional.

Now, I realize only a few people in the wrestling business will get this and understand this because those that get it, well, they get it and understand it. The problem is there are guys in the back who should be buying a ticket to the show and have no reason to even be booked on the show. They are the ones who won't get this or understand this, because they are the very same guys who already know everything. I always forget most of these guys who I see doing these idiotic things at these small independent shows already know everything. Again, this isn't meant for any certain one indie group and at no one in particular, but if I were in charge of a locker room or was a booker for the show, there's no way in hell a couple of these guys would ever work on my show or any other show that I had any influence over. Some of you know–it–alls, and trust me, I don't know everything, I still learn all the time, the business changes, people, the boys, the fans, they change, and I get that, but the biggest problem is, some of you dip shits already know everything because you have to get your shit in, and are happy working for free or for that cold hot dog, left over flat soda pop, and stale popcorn, all the while telling your friends and neighbors, "Hey I'm a pro rassler." No! You're not! You're an idiot who is killing the professional wrestling business.

Professionals get paid. Every other major sport including WWE, TNA, ROH, NJPW, and countless other companies and organizations pay their employees, and their employees conduct themselves as professionals.

One quality that does matter in regards to having a locker room with a leader in it is that of loyalty. You want to have loyalty, but you, as a locker room leader should also be willing to be loyal to the boys under you as well. You have to put personal feelings aside and be a professional about some things when it comes to locker room loyalty. There are many times, more often than not when loyalty can overcome a person's flaws.

## ✥ Questionable Tactics ✥

I've met plenty of referees through the years and some of the fans don't understand just how important a referee's job is inside the squared circle. This doesn't bother me, as some of the fans are, "in the know" if you will, due to the business of professional wrestling being exposed like it has been through the years. However, what does bother me is when one or some of the green boys or "wrestlers," and I'll use that term gingerly here, don't get it or don't understand or appreciate just how important it is to have a knowledgeable ref on any professional show. In the words of Jim Cornette, as stated in his book, *Rags, Paper, and Pins*, "The most maligned, thankless job in wrestling is that of the referee. But, it's a necessary job, and there would be no matches without them. So even though a referee may not always see every infraction of the rules, these men deserve thanks from both the wrestlers and the fans."

Having a quality ref on the show can make or break a match or the entire show depending on whether or not he's been trained and or smartened up to the wrestling business. You don't go to an NBA basketball game and see amateurs out there refereeing the games, you see professionals. The same can be said for MLB, the NHL, or even take a look back when the NFL had to use "replacement refs" during part of the year a few seasons back. This should show you how important a ref's job is, whether it is on a field, court, or at a live pro wrestling event. So, with that in mind, what makes someone, and I'm strictly talking about an independent wrestling show, think they can use an untrained ref on the show? A better question may be what if you have a trained qualified professional referee on the show who has more knowledge than some of the goofs working the show?

31

There's a huge advantage to having a smart qualified ref on the show.

Many fans know some if not all of the refs they see week in and week out on the national level, so I'll spare all the name dropping, but will mention only two. I'll mention these two, as I know each of them first hand and can attest to their knowledge and understanding of the wrestling business before going into further detail about having non-trained or bad refs on a show.

I was in Charlotte, North Carolina on the night Charles Robinson had his tryout for WCW. He was there on the same night I had my tryout. Charles had a good look to him, I'm sure he was a little nervous, and who wouldn't be? But, he also had all the confidence in the world that he was going to go out to the ring and do his job that evening as ref and hopefully secure himself a spot on the WCW roster, and he did. He quickly advanced through the ranks of WCW as a ref and eventually secured a job with the WWE.

He knew and understood his job before he ever even got a tryout with a major company. He also continued to learn, work hard, and do what was asked of him in performing his job as a professional referee. Look at where he is at today. He's still there in the WWE today after all these years and does a fantastic job.

Charles is a prime example of how hard work pays off if you're willing to work hard to succeed in doing something you love. Mike Mooneyham, of *The Post and Courier* in Charleston, South Carolina has called Charles Robinson, "The hardest working man in WWE." Way to go Charles!

Again, you can go back through the years of whatever wrestling program you happened to watch back in the day and probably name more refs than I can. A couple of names that come to my mind are the names Jerry Calhoun and Paul Morton, as they were the two I saw the most being brought up on the old Memphis Wrestling back in the day. Tommy Young is another name that also comes to my mind as one of the all-time greats that I recall seeing once I started watching the National Wrestling Alliance on TV.

Another nationally known referee who I will mention is WWE ref Scott Armstrong. Scott was raised in the business.

Scott was a wonderfully talented wrestler back in the day and has landed a great job with WWE as a ref. I'm sure there are many more reasons than I know as to why he has a job with the WWE, but the main one is because he gets and understands his job as a ref and understands the professional wrestling business. Scott now serves as a road agent and producer for the WWE. Scott is another great example of hard work paying off and bringing success. I merely mention these two gentlemen out of respect for each and to also illustrate the point that they are trained professionals. They get it! When you hear the little announcement at the beginning of your most recent WWE DVD that says, "Don't try this at home," well that goes for trying to referee as well. Refereeing a professional match is a complicated business. Leave it to the professionals!

So, where am I going with this story about referees? I'll give you a couple of illustrations. Frankie Reyes, who I mentioned in my first book, is a first class referee. I worked along with Frankie from helping him set up the ring to training other students back in the days of our training at Malenko's. Frankie has refereed matches for all the major companies in his thirty plus years. He is always willing to help give young guys pointers as they are learning to wrestle while still refereeing and helping veterans work out finishes for their matches. We traveled to Australia together and while we were there, he refereed every match, every night, and never forgot a finish. He was and is what one would call, "A complete professional."

David Webb is a friend of mine who used to work out at the YMCA and refereed everything starting with high school football, basketball, and baseball games. He even made it all the way up to AAA baseball in the majors. He used to ref several shows in addition to other duties on the local shows I had with my old company Championship Pro Wrestling. He knew how to work along with the guys and along with the crowd to add to the excitement of the matches. He really sold all the moves a lot like Mark Curtis did in SMW. Dave even filled in on several occasions on some SMW shows when they were in the area. All he needed to be told was a finish and he would take care of the rest in the ring, and with great professionalism I might add.

A ref has to know when to count, how quick to get down on the mat to count, when to see certain things and when not to see certain things. It's important for a ref to understand this. On one such occasion in my second match with Dan "The Beast" Severn, we had a different ref from Mark Curtis. The story of my second match with Dan can be read elsewhere in the book, but for the sake of how important it is to know your ref or for him to know his job, I'll use this little part of the match right here. The match was in Knoxville. This match was an overall good match, one I consider much better than the first match we had only a few months prior.

The bell rings, and I still don't know who this ref is to this day, but it's not Mark Curtis. The opening sequence was going to be me taking Severn down in a quick fireman's carry for a quick pin, and then he would do the same to me, again for a quick pin to show the quickness of each, and how competitive the match was going to be between us. The fireman's carry was executed, perfectly, I might add by myself and of course by world class wrestler Severn. Well, as quick as we did the moves, the ref was just getting down for the second fireman carry and gave a half–assed one count before Severn and I were back to our feet and shaking hands out of respect for each other's wrestling skills. I have no doubt that had Curtis or another more competent ref been in that ring then the first two quick fireman's carries with a quick pin and a quick count by the ref would have come off a lot better than it did.

It would have been so much more beautiful and made so much more sense to help with the flow of the match and the story we were going to be telling through our match. After that, Severn and I just worked our match and went on as if the ref wasn't there and worked and finished our match. Again, I'll go into more match detail elsewhere. But, the point I'm making is the ref was not experienced enough or was just too damned lazy to get his butt down on the mat to make the quick counts to make the opening spot look spectacular rather than regular.

With the above story or illustrations let me leave you with one more thought about how important a referee is to the show. Other than being responsible for all the finishes and remembering each or helping by being in the right place at the right time and such, think about how an experienced ref can add to story lines and help a wrestler, be it a baby face or a heel. Hell do they even have baby faces and heels in pro wrestling anymore? But, I digress. Dan Marsh was a former wrestler turned referee when I worked back in the old Gran Prix territory when I was first breaking into the business. His knowledge for the business and as a ref was unequaled when it came to helping maintain order in the ring and helping the greener guys, including myself to learn, know, and understand just how important the ref was and is to the matches. I learned a lot from him.

Now, again, I'm talking about independent wrestling and in this case back when wrestling had territories. It's important that the ref kept up with each performer or wrestler's gimmick when they had weekly programs and sold programs at the shows or still had newspaper coverage of the week's events and matches.

Mary Bond was one such newspaper reporter who always kept all the fans in the know about what matches were coming to what town, and also which wrestlers were facing each other in the upcoming weeks. She also did a wonderful job of giving the guys coverage through interviews she ran in the paper as well as in the weekly programs during the shows.

So, let's get on with the story. A green guy or in this case a guy who says he has been everywhere and wrestled everyone, when in reality he was a, "40 miler." For you that don't know what a "40 miler" is, it's a guy who has never wrestled anywhere further than a forty mile radius of his home town, and more than likely only had a few matches per year and yet claims to have wrestled the world over. So the guy says to Dan, "What do you know? You're just a ref." Yes, he is a ref, but he isn't just a referee. He's a guy who has been all over the US and Canada and even refereed for the old WWF back in the day. Think about how much he actually did know. Wow, if only some of these guys would take the time to listen to someone like that, then maybe they would begin to understand the importance of having a good quality ref on hand for the show.

Here's an example: The newspaper article and the wrestling program said, "Bobby Blaze has talent as a skilled wrestler but he has been known to use questionable tactics." So what was my response? "Questionable tactics? Hey, ask the ref! I'm an honest man. Why would I lie or ever think about using questionable tactics? I don't need to cheat to win my matches." Now, if the ref, knows that I have been heeling out, or using these so called questionable tactics, the heat's on him. We weren't trying to get the heat on the ref. The fans and the baby face wrestlers all had been accusing me of throwing a fireball into my opponent's face. Of course, I had been known to do so back when I worked in this territory. It was a part of my gimmick and at this point a part of our angle. But, had he seen these things or even let on to the fans that he wasn't on the up and up, then it just kills not only the show, but probably the whole town and maybe other towns as well, as word gets around.

He has to let the fans know that he is an honest referee and would be certain to keep a closer eye on these so called "bad guys" using questionable tactics. He has to be smart in order to play dumb. After all you can't put the heat on the referee unless that's a small part of the program, so he must be certain that he plays his role, or uses his gimmick in this case, as a ref to the fullest. JJ Dillion may have said it best, "A good referee is someone who is there, but also someone who is not there. They take steps to be sure they don't become the focus of attention. A good referee is worth his weight in gold, because he knows how to give the impression that he's somebody."

So the newspaper and program further goes on to say, "The referee, a former WWF referee even said, 'I've been involved in thousands of matches through the years. I know my job. I've refereed many of Bobby's matches over the course of two years, and I have never seen Bobby cheat or use questionable tactics.'"

So, you see how this works? If you're a young guy or still green, listen to the referee. Mark Curtis was one of the first guys I got close to back when I started with SMW as he, as a ref had his finger on the pulse of what was happening in the territory. Most refs know what's going on before the boys do in many cases. Listen to them. If you're new at refereeing, keep learning, know the rules, watch other sports and see how the referees there conduct themselves. Commit yourself to excellence! You have to learn! Promoters make sure you have a skilled, trained, professional referee in order to run an organized professional wrestling show.

I've said it before and I'll say it again, I don't care how many people you draw to your building or arena, you give the fans their money's worth. In fact you'll be far better off if you give each fan more than their money's worth, and more than likely, those fans, and many more will be at your next event or show. So, always realize that having a professional referee is a part of your show. Plus, if I'm in the match, highly unlikely at this point, but nonetheless, if I've got my shoulders to the mat, and as I watch the refs hand coming down for that three count, I can kick out on two. My timing with Mark Curtis was remarkable and I always knew exactly when to bridge up or kick my legs so I would kick out on two at the last possible moment. That's part of what makes pro wrestling exciting, seeing a guy kick out on two!

## ❧ Four ❧

## ❧ The People I Meet...My Dark Places ❧

I meet people. I meet people from all walks of life. Sometimes I meet these people in dark places. Sometimes we lift each other up. Sometimes I'm lifted up by seeing and using the darkness they live in. There was this one time in a dimly lit motel room when I met such a person. It was a motel room, not a hotel room. And believe you me, there's a difference, because a good hoe don't tell, but I digress. Anyway, you lift that person out of that gutter, and out of that dark place and it's at that moment when she jumps up on the bed in that room and breaks out in song, to which the lyrics I do not know, but her voice is carrying in a way, like the wings on a bird, her soul sings...that's a good place to be. Savior, survivor, rescuer, it's a role to which I have become accustomed, because I have been where that person was. The key is to not stay in the darkness or let the one that is down keep you down. "Well, I've been so Goddamn down, that it looks like up to me," those words by Jim Morrison and The Doors echo through my head as I think about how dark my place can be. Like I said, I have been there too, my friend, and it's not a place to be. That's why when I go into my darkest places...I somehow always seem to find the light, or maybe the light finds me, it's because I meet people...

*"Sometimes I sleep, sometimes it's not for days*
*The people I meet always go their separate ways*
*Sometimes you tell the day*
*By the bottle that you drink*
*And times when you're all alone all you do is think"*
*Bon Jovi*

## ❧ Famous People ❧

Celebrities, yeah I've met a few. Through years of wrestling and traveling throughout the world I met a lot of famous people other than professional wrestlers. Entertainers, you probably know. The list includes actors, singers, comedians, and other sports figures. I've never been much on getting autographs or having my picture taken with famous people, as to that, I just rely on my memory. But, as I recently told a group of young wrestlers one night over dinner, "Get every autograph you can, and have your picture made with other wrestlers if you have the chance." Personally, for the most part I couldn't care less about meeting famous people or celebrities, but that may only be because I've met my fair share. I told the youngsters at the table that night to get those autographs and pictures because of social media. I didn't tell them that so much for the memories, but with the explosion of social media, which I think is pretty damn cool, Twitter, FaceBook, and Instagram just to

*Yours Truly with Mrs. Foley's little boy and Momma Cornette's son*

name a few, gives the world a chance to see who you met in the zoo, and to see who's who.

In addition to all the famous people I've met from my home town, in the, "Achy Breaky HOF" section and a few more that I didn't list, here's just a couple of other celebrities I've met through the years. In no certain or chronological order, here's the rich and famous of who's who in the zoo. "Lifestyles of the rich and famous, They're always complainin' Always complainin' If money is such problem, You've got so many problems, Think I could solve them, Lifestyles of the rich and famous," Lyrics credit goes to Good Charlotte of course.

Mayhem! Yeah that may have been the way things seemed in WCW at times, but they were at one point winning the Monday Night Wrestling Wars in the ratings. Of course many on the inside who may have thought that this would go on forever were only being delusional if they thought that VKM and the WWE was just going to throw in the towel. As we all know by now, that wasn't the case, and now VKM and his billion dollar company now own all the rights to everything that was WCW and got it all for pennies on the dollar. Anyway, there's a brief free history lesson, and if you want to learn or know more about it, it's all detailed out on the internet on several sites and on DVD's. Spoiler Alert! There was a downfall!

WCW was however trying to do new things and one of the things they tried to do was stay involved in the video game market. The company that they partnered up with for this endeavor was EA Sports. EA Sports, "It's in the Game" is a brand of video game publisher Electronic Arts which develops sports video games and this was to be their first attempt at doing one based on professional wrestling. They were already known for doing sports video games for NASCAR, NHL, and of course Madden NFL.

I was selected to go to the offices in Vancouver, British Columbia, Canada to be a part of this ground breaking sports video game. EA Sports is a first class company. They treated myself and Bobby Eaton, Buddy Lee Parker, and Lash Larue with style and kept it first class. Each day we were picked up by limousine from The Pacific Palisades Hotel and Resort, where each of us had our own town house condo. Every day! It took us to the sports arena to do the motion capture that would include over 600 wrestling moves and holds and then back again in the evening.

One evening we were having dinner when in walks the very sexy Sara Jessica Parker. She probably is best known for her leading role as Carrie Bradshaw on the HBO television series *Sex and the City*. She was in town, and staying in the same hotel. She was leading a production meeting the best we could tell. She sure was pretty and she was stacked, if you know what I mean, and I'm sure you do. I'm a leg and thigh man myself, but on that night the breast was looking mighty tasty. I ordered chicken breast.

On another night while sitting down to dinner, my chair was up against a chair at another table. It just so happened to be Justine Bateman. She is best known for her role as Mallory Keaton on the sitcom *Family Ties*. Justine and I actually played a game of pretend flirting as we were seated back to back and kept bumping chair backs. I can think of

40

some other bumping I would have rather been doing but her brother, Jason, didn't seem too amused. He was actually pretty cool but seemed to be in a more serious mood than his sister. She started it out as a slow and seductive tease with some little accidental bumps and some not so innocent giggles. After a couple more drinks, needless to say, it didn't take me long to start bumping back into her chair. She was game for it. So, every once in a while, while the other was taking a bite of food or trying to get a drink the other would " accidentally" scoot back or ease their chair back just a little to make each other miss their mouths. All in all it was just innocent fun, but, truthfully I wouldn't have minded a little "family ties" fun.

The next two men are now deceased but they both were known throughout the world in their respective fields as legends. As I said, I rarely have asked others for autographs but there was one I wish I had gotten, if not for me, but for my dad. I shared a train/tram ride in Orlando out to our flight to Charlotte and I wish I would have gotten an autograph from Dale Earnhardt Sr. He had just competed in The Daytona 500. He looked tired and worn out. I was just coming off of a ten day tour of Florida. He probably didn't know who I was but he could probably tell that I was a pro wrestler. I'm sure the Gold's Gym tank top, the tan, and bleached blond hair were a sure giveaway. One thing for sure, I damn sure knew who he was. After all, he was, "The Intimidator." Sadly two years later he died in a crash at Daytona. I don't think too much about not getting his autograph, but I do often wish that Earnhardt was still with us to see him in victory lane one more time.

Leslie Nielsen, I'm sure I met him. "Surely you can't be serious." "I am serious...and don't call me Shirley." What a great actor and comedian. He appeared in more than 100 films and 1500 television programs, portraying more than 220 characters. Leslie Nielsen was also staying at the Pacific Palisades in Vancouver, Canada at the same time as me and the guys I've already mentioned were. While having our morning breakfast, out of nowhere in walks Mr. Nielsen.

He walked like he had been in a few professional wrestling matches himself. WOW! I had seen him in so many of his films such as *Airplane*, *Naked Gun*, and *Dracula: Dead*

41

*and Loving It*, and *Mr. Magoo*. I think he was there shooting, the movie *Wrongfully Accused* in Vancouver, when I met him. After ordering coffee and flirting with the waitress he realized that the four big guys at the next table were all smiling and whispering under their breath as to who he was. He graciously introduced himself and said, "I figured you guys were fighters or bouncers or something." Upon learning that we were wrestlers he really started hamming it up. He was entertaining us, his table guest and his cute waitress throughout breakfast. It was fun talking to him and listening to him through the entire breakfast. That's the kind of memory that you don't need to have an autograph or photograph to remember. I was there!

There are many more famous people and other celebrities that I've met through the years. Some, I'd just see at airports or at a hotel, sometimes I'd just give them a nod or they would look in my direction, nonetheless, I never tried to bother them with getting a picture taken or asking for an autograph. That's just not my style. And, really, at the end of the day, many are just like you and me, well, um, except they're rich and famous.

## ∾ Achy Breaky Hall of Fame ∾

Many times out on the road when guys are telling stories or telling jokes, pulling ribs, counting crows, you know, just to keep from being bored to death on long car rides, the topic of our home town, "Hall of Fame" would come up. Now this was before the WWE had a HOF and if you're into that kind of thing, that's cool, and if not, well, you'll probably appreciate this story all the more.

Speaking of the WWE HOF, there are many great men who have been left off the list, and even many more who deserve to be in every professional HOF that ever existed. This is not a dig on what most people see each year on the annual event put on by the WWE, as I think it's a fantastic event. I think it's great for the business, for the boys, and more importantly for the fans. Sadly, most of these fans have been force fed what they see and believe and have little actual knowledge of some of the true greats that have graced the squared circle. Here's your disclaimer, if you like

Sports Entertainment™, good for you, if you like pro wrestling, even better because again, you will remember and know who rightfully belongs in these HOF's. I, for the record will never be in the WWE HOF. I have no grand illusion about this fact. That's kind of the gist of the story; guys like me can't even get into our home town HOF.

I'll put the car in reverse for a minute. On the long road trips, whether in a car, in the back of a ring truck, on a bus, or even on a plane you have to break up the travel with jokes, stories, and ribs. Sometimes you make up or play silly games. I mentioned counting crows above. When I was traveling up in Canada, and sometimes while in SMW or working on indie shows we played, "Crows." We, being whoever was in the car, usually 4–5 guys, would write down a number and initial it and place it in the glove box along with two or three dollars each. We were making a wager on the number of crows we would spot going from one town to the next. At night, sometimes we played, "Deer." Anyway, everyone had a number written down, and depending on the length of the trip, pretty day, rainy day etc., you would wager.

Side bets could be made between guys on an over or under on say 100 crows or such, and if someone had the exact number that was actually seen by all passengers, everyone paid the winner double. It wasn't much, but it was fun, and you might actually win six to fifteen dollars or enough to pay for a meal or towards the gas chip in. By the way, dead crows don't count! Rico, Eddie, Cuban or anyone else who played this game would beg to differ. Heels! Y'all were always looking for ways to cheat; but isn't that the way it should be for a heel? Ha-ha. Again, it was just a fun way to pass time. This now brings us to another game. As we spoke about our hometowns, we would play the, "Hall of Fame" game.

I've played the HOF Game with many guys through the years. The original crew that used to play it with me back in the day was Dan Marsh, Todd MacPhee, Robert Maillet, and a young Indian boy I only knew as, "Soaring Eagle." Dan would joke that the rock-n-roll group Rush was from Toronto and that they would kill his chances of ever getting in.

Well Dan, now you'll have to get in line behind Mike Myers, Drake, and maybe even Rob Ford, that is if he isn't in one of his drunken stupors. Todd MacPhee, it seems Ann Murray was and is your only competition from Springhill, Nova Scotia, Canada, so good luck on getting in. Soaring Eagle, you made your people proud of you. You just might have a chance.

But, the one who has the best and biggest chance of being into their Hometown Hall of Fame is none other than Robert "The Acadian Giant" Maillet. Many may remember him as Kurrgan during his WWF/WWE run. He may even have a chance to one day be inducted into the WWE HOF. He is the really big guy who has been in movies like *Sherlock Holmes*, *300*, *Pacific Rim,* and *Hercules*. He's also been in, *The Strain* on Syfy TV and many other roles in the movies and television shows. He may get his own Star on The Hollywood Walk of Fame. We are all so proud of you and your accomplishments. I could go on and on listing names that have played the HOF Game through the years but I think you, my dear reader, get the gist of it.

Coming from Ashland, Kentucky I have many people from my hometown to compete with. It's surprising how many famous people came from such a small town that sits on the banks of the Ohio River. I'm competing against the likes of baseball great Brandon Webb. I mean this guy only pitched his way into winning the 2006 National League Cy Young award in the MLB. By the way, Brandon is a great guy and a fine example of how an athlete should conduct his life when off the field. I'm always happy to shake his hand from time to time when we pass each other at the store.

Keep in mind; I was playing this game with my buddies when another guy with a mullet was making trips back and forth to Nashville, Tennessee trying to catch a break in country music. You may have heard of him, if not, I'm sure you've heard of his daughter, Miley. Billy Ray, oh my! My *Achy Breaky Heart* is breaking as my chances of ever getting into my hometown HOF just keep getting slimmer and slimmer.

I don't want to leave anyone out, but I'll mention a few to prove just what I was up against on these trips. Maybe you've heard of Allison Anders. She's a famous director,

44

writer, and producer out in Hollywood, and good for her and her much deserved success. She's also the half–sister of a couple of my good friends, Dirk Anders and Bob Anders. Hey guys, get her to get us in a movie. I need the money.

I mentioned The Country Music Highway, route 23 running right through my county, well; the section near me is known as, "Judd Highway." Yep, I have The Judd's, to compete with, and that was back before Ashley started making a name for herself as an established movie star and number one UK fan. They are all nice ladies and still come back home at times to help with local charities and food drives. I sure do wish Ashley would have warmed up to me one evening on a late flight. That would have been sweet. I guess the mile high club thought still drives me a little bit nuts...and to think. Oh never mind.

There's a street named after Chuck Woolery. Many know him from being a famous game show host. I met him at the YMCA when he was home to be the Grand Marshall of the Ashland Christmas Parade. He had his wife with him at the time, not sure which one, but she was stacked. Her surgeon, whoever he was, deserves a huge bonus. I was just thinking the entire time she was working out; "If I could just have 'two minutes and two seconds'" we might just have a little love connection.

There have been many more good people that have come from Ashland, Kentucky. There's been plenty of other baseball players like Billy and Bob Lynch, Don Robinson, and Drew Hall. Two others, Charlie Reliford and Greg Gibson are both umpires in Major League Baseball. I've personally met, or know all the ones I've mentioned and believe me this is just a small number of people that, if there ever were a local HOF they would be elected to it before I would.

Sonny Landham was on several TV shows and a bunch of movies, including a couple he did with Arnold Schwarzengger. There's also radio personality and singer, Julie Reeves, as well as the late great Keith Whitley.

There's also many great teachers and coaches that could make it into my hometown HOF. My vote goes to Coach Herb Conley! He was a great football player and coach and far more deserving than myself.

Then of course there's Charles Manson. How the hell can I compete with that nut? I'll never even make it on the ballot with all these famous people and celebrities being from Ashland.

Well at least I'm mentioned on the Ashland, Kentucky Wikipedia page under, "Notable People."

*Ashland Kentucky, AKA "Parts Unknown"*

## ✌ Five ☙

*"Tryin' to make a livin' and doing the best I can...and when it's time for leavin' I hope you'll understand, I was born a ramblin' man."—The Allman Brothers Band*

When it's time to hit the road, it's time to crank up the music. Everyone has to have a great bunch of songs to jam to while out on the road. If you're in the car with a great bunch of fellas, just roll down the windows, turn up the music, and hit the cruise control. Okay, leave the windows up; it might be a cold winter day, either way, crank up that damn road music.

The music I listen to and jam to while traveling may not be for you, and yours may not be for me, but there is a large stable of guys who will agree on several great songs that should be on everyone's play list. This little list of songs is in no certain order. Anyone who has ever wrestled or traveled in planes, trains, and automobiles probably has a similar play list as well.

Everyone has those special songs, those special moments of being in a car and then that one special song comes on, and you just turn it up. You can love all kinds of music and depending on the song it just takes you to a special place in your mind. You don't have to be a wrestler to get or understand the songs I'm going to list, but I think a vast majority of the boys will agree on most of the ones I selected. Awe, the memories. Hit my music!

*Here I Go Again*, White Snake. Okay, stop thinking about Tawny Kitaen on the hood of a car in a white dress and just listen to the song. "An' I've made up my mind, and I ain't wasting no more time, but here I go again, here I go again."

Turn it up! *Sweet Home Alabama*, Lynyrd Skynyrd. "Big wheels keep on turning, carrying me home to see my kin..." It doesn't matter if it's the wheels of a car, a train, or a tour bus in some foreign land, man, sometimes you just got to hope those wheels keep turning to get you home to see your family. Hey, I dated a girl from Alabama once, just once, uh, never mind, turn this one up real loud.

*King Of The Road*, Roger Miller. Hey, it's an oldie but a goldie. But then again, all my songs are oldies. I find this one a good comparison to Jack Kerouac's classic novel, *On the Road*, even though it was published in 1957, and the song didn't come out until 1964, it just puts you in that state of mind about traveling across America. Check it out sometime when you have nothing better to do than drive.

The Doors are one of my favorites, if not my all-time favorite band, so *Riders on the Storm* has to be on my list. I mean, "There's a killer on the road, his brain is squirmin' like a toad" for goodness sakes. Don't give this man a ride. There's a rider on a storm out there and the world on you depends. What? Get me home!

Anyone whose driven cross country knows there are a lot of good songs out there that are a must. You don't even have to like punk music to enjoy, *Should I Stay or Should I Go*, by The Clash. It's just a good rockin' song, period! Hell, London could be calling for all I care, I just know I like jamming out to it.

Whether you're traveling to a town to wrestle or going to a town on a vacation, sometimes it's all about escape. Even the towns one may be wishing or desiring to escape from are the towns that we might be wrestling in on any given night. So, this next one, *Born To Run*, by "The Boss" Bruce Springsteen is a great song about getting out of where you're at. Just hit track number five on your cassette or CD and, "Baby this town rips the bones from your back, it's a death trap, a suicide rap...we gotta get out while we're young...Baby we were born to run..."

Whoa, all I want is, *On the Road Again*. Let Willie Nelson tell you about life on tour. Every night you're in a different town and in a different venue. It's a life where, every day is a holiday, every meal a banquet, and a life better than the president. I can't wait to get on the road again.

"Up with the sun, gone with the wind...feelin' the breeze, passing the cars..." *Travelin' Man* by Bob Seger is one killer song. Just take the time to listen and enjoy...and..."Those are the memories that made me a wealthy soul."

Meeting girls and good times in every town, every night, tell me where to sign up please. The Allman Brothers Band sure knew all about it in, *Ramblin' Man*. If you're going to rock out going down the highway this one is a must have

48

especially if you're in the wrestling business because we're all just, "Tryin' to make a livin' and doing the best I can...and when it's time for leavin' I hope you'll understand, I was born a ramblin' man."

This next one may not be on everyone's play list but it certainly is on mine, *Runnin' Down a Dream*. Even though I had been wrestling since 1988, when this song came out in July of 89' "I felt so good, like anything was possible," once I had started my training at Malenko's the previous month. Like the song says, "I was runnin' down a dream, that never would come to me."

Who can forget when big ol' Dusty Rhodes got suspended and had to leave a town or territory when out of nowhere and usually within a few days, "The Midnight Rider" would show up? Even though the song wasn't actually about Dusty and had nothing to do with wrestling, it's a great road song, and great song about having to get away. The Allman Brothers Band classic, *Midnight Rider* is just that, classic. "And I don't own the clothes I'm wearing...and the road goes on forever...and I'm not gonna let em' catch the midnight rider."

Whew, with all the running down of dreams, and not letting people catch you, sometimes you just feel like you're, *Running on Empty*. Jackson Browne sure knew about, "Looking back at the years gone by like so many summer fields." Just like the song says, "I'd love to stick around, but I'm running behind...I'm running on empty."

Alright now, even though, we're getting close to our destinations, or feeling like we are running on empty, professional wrestlers, ticket sellers, custodians, ring crews, bus drivers, and anyone else involved in the business knows it's time to load out and go. *The Load Out* and *Stay*, again by Jackson Browne, brings out the best in all of us. We hopefully have given all the great fans one great match or one of the absolute best professional wrestling shows ever witnessed, and we may be tired and worn plumb out, but deep down, we wish we could just, "Stay" a little bit longer. Onstage, backstage, in the ring, it doesn't get any better than this right here. It's all about the scene that's going on man. It's all around you in and on every professionally promoted show in the world. "Pack it up, and tear it down...they'll set it up in another town..." Yes, I realize it's basically two songs, I think it's meant to be played as one, but once I get back into my car or climb back on that bus, "these towns all look the same...and we hear that crowd, and we remember why we came..."

That makes it all worthwhile. Every ache, pain, worry, or care in the world all vanishes once we hit that ring to perform for our fans. "Oh, won't you stay just a little bit longer, please, please, please say you will, say you will...Stay!"

And finally..."On a long and lonesome highway, East of Omaha, You can listen to the engine, Moan' out his one note song, You can think about the woman, or the girl you knew the night before..." There's really no explanation needed or required, *Turn the Page*, by Bob Seger. "There I go again...Turn the page..."

## ❧ Save Your Money ❧

"Save your money kid, I've seen your show." No matter what job you ever get or have, and especially in professional wrestling, save your money. There's an old saying in the business about seeing your show or your act, and believe me when your time is up and you're no longer bringing in a check or money from wrestling, you will be broke. Trust me on this, I know. "It's not how much money you make, it's how much money you save." I wish I had listened to the countless veterans who told me this throughout the years. They, well, many of them knew way more than I did about the importance of saving your money. The money won't last forever and that's a straight shoot.

Through the years, I tried to live frugally while on the road. Even when I was making good money, I tried my best to keep it simple in my meals and road expenses. I've heeled hotel rooms, sleeping four or five guys to a room, and even slept ass cheek to ass cheek with a former NWA Heavyweight Champion. Oh, here we go with another crazy story. Well, it's not as crazy as it sounds. I used to pick up Tommy "Wildfire" Rich at the airport in Cleveland, Ohio when we used to work for CAPW. If you've read, *Pin Me Pay Me* then you'll know I loved working for JT Lightning and with his crew of guys there. So anyway, a couple of times someone would just give us the money to go out to get our hotel room on our own if JT or Big Josh hadn't already reserved a room for us. Tommy and I went to the show after me picking him up and then proceeded down to where we had been told a room would be paid for. Well we got there and there was a communication problem with the reservations. We called JT and he sent someone down and gave Tommy and myself ninety dollars each to cover the rooms. While sitting out in the car thinking and talking, an idea came to us in a puff of smoke. Why not just get one room, share it, and split the extra money?

I thought it was a good idea and proceeded to go in and get the room. I told Tommy they only had one room with one queen size bed, and I could sleep on the floor or we could split it with one of us getting box springs and the other get the mattress. "I don't mind sleeping ass cheek to ass cheek if you don't" is what I believe Tommy said. So we gathered our gear went to the room, split the money, and crashed out.

Forty five dollars each for the next three nights wasn't a bad gimmick. Who wouldn't want an extra $135.00 for meals and other consumables while doing a loop with a former world champion? I always got along great with Tommy. We didn't do that every trip together but we shared many rooms together and it was always fun. Anyway, that's that, I did save money when I could.

One of the funniest stories about trying to save money happened when I was in WCW. I have stayed at a lot of nice hotels throughout my career, but again, the object was to try to save some money when you could, so at times I may have stayed at a lesser known motel chain rather than a nicer or finer hotel. Hey, if it had four walls, a TV, and a bed I was fine with it. That doesn't include the motel that I stayed in somewhere around Boone, North Carolina and a bullet came through one of my walls after the couple next door had been arguing for a couple hours. Shit happens, I get it. Just like I packed my shit and got out of there and drove as far as I could until I found a rest area to finish up my night of sleep.

Anyway, back to the days of WCW. Barry Horowitz was one of the best at knowing what gyms in each town were free to work out in, which hotels had the best rates, and what car rental services offered the best daily or weekly rates. Barry was another Malenko guy like me. We both always got along just fine with each other and I had a lot of respect for him. He had made a career out of being pinned and getting people over for a long time. He was one of the best at doing his job, and doing it well.

His story could have been *Pin Me Pay Me* because he even put me over in Corpus Christi, Texas when I kicked out on two and got him with a surprise Northern Lights Suplex. Thanks Barry. But, there was one place I could never beat Barry, and that was when it came to getting a better rate on a hotel or a rental car. Even when I thought I had him beat one time, he got the last laugh in on me.

Even though I can recall the town where I went over on him, I can't remember the town where he really got one over on me. During catering, many times he and I would share stories about what hotel we had gotten and at what rate. He willingly shared information with me about the different towns and cities that he had long worked and knew all the best rates as I said. Well anyhow, I walked up to the Avis counter at some airport in some town and gave the man my name and reservation. When the guy turned to look at the envelopes with the names on them that contained the car keys I noticed one that said, Horowitz, B. When the guy turned around and handed me the key and asked for my credit card, I sensed that the guy was of good nature and kidded around with him for a second or two and asked him if he could do me a favor. At the time I had an Avis card and always got rentals pretty cheap on their small or economy cars if I was traveling alone.

One this day, my rate was only going to be $14.99 plus tax. I asked the guy if he could check the price that Horowitz was getting and if so, could he please rent me the car for at least one cent cheaper than whatever his price was. I explained that I knew him, and we were trying to always out do or in this case pay less or get something cheaper than the other. The guy said that his rate was basically the same as mine and he could even do better than my one cent request due to the taxes and everything being in the computer already, he would rent me my car for only $14.95, a full four cents cheaper than the one on reserve for Horowitz. B. Man,

I had him. He hadn't picked up his reservation yet. I couldn't wait to get to building to tell Barry when he got there that I finally got him; I finally beat him on the price of something, even if it was only four cents. Sometimes on the road, it's the little things.

I get to the arena, drop off my gear in the dressing area and proceed on over to catering to have my evening meal. It was a day just like any other day, except today, I was going to rib Barry about my huge savings on my car rental when he got there. As I walked into the catering area I see Barry is already at a table eating. I didn't give it a second thought. I didn't even wonder how he had beaten me to the arena even though I had picked up my car first. I was just excited to know I finally was going to have some bragging rights over him on the car rental. I went up to prepare my plate, get my drink and then head over to where Barry was. I sat my tray down with a smile on my face. Before I even sat down with the group of guys where Barry was eating, I said something to the effect of, "I finally got ya Horowitz. I beat ya on the car rental today at Avis. I only paid $14.95 for my car and I know yours was $14.99." He just smiled, then literally laughed out loud as he said, "Sorry Buddy, I didn't get my rental from there today. I went over to the Budget counter and they gave me one for $13.99 so I rented from them." Not only did he laugh again, several others including myself laughed as well. I may have kicked out on two and got that one win on him in the ring, but by God, I sure as hell couldn't beat him anywhere else, especially when it came to saving money on the road. So, the moral of the story, "Save your money kid. It won't last forever."

## ❧ Universal Studios ❧

### & Thursday Night Thunder

You know, at one point in my wrestling career, I used to get to go to Universal Studios in Orlando, Florida for free. WCW did their World Wide Wrestling Television taping there. It was always a fun trip for me. We would tape for ten days at the theme park and while we were there we had a full access pass. It was really cool that when you weren't wrestling you could just go out into the park, walk around, hang out, or even go right to the front of the line and ride any ride you wanted. Talk about a great job perk.

Anyway, on most of the World Wide tapings I usually went over on whoever I was wrestling with, with the exception of a couple of guys. One of the guys that I put over was Brian "Crush" Adams. He had just come into WCW off a recent run with the WWE and was going to get a strong push. I think he did a match with Bret Hart or maybe a run in and attacked him the night before but either way he was just about ready to get a push with the then red hot NWO.

The first day he showed up for the World Wide tapings we were going to work together. He approached me in a very professional manner and asked me if I could make him look good and keep him strong during the match. I told him of course I could. I'm not so sure he believed me or thought I could, as he didn't know me and had never worked with me before. It was just something I sensed during our brief talk. The tapings there usually aired over the course of the next three months and then we would return and tape another three months worth. I'm just pointing this out, because we really never knew when the show would air, but since he was just coming in, he knew he had to stay strong whether it aired the following week or three months down the line. Anyway, he came back over to me about fifteen or twenty minutes later and wanted to know if he could speak to me in private. I told him sure and we kind of walked off to the side of one of the large recording studios. He said, "Hey, I just spoke with Dean Malenko and he told me not to worry about anything that you were a hell of a hand. I hope you didn't mind." "Of course not, I'll do whatever you wanna do and give you a good match. I'm easy to work with." Again, all this was very professional, as he asked me if I minded if he press slammed me somewhere in the match. Again, it was no problem for me. It's business only. He just said, "Well you call it out there and when it's right hit the ropes and when you come off that's when I'll know you're ready to go up and then we'll go into my finish." I knew when he walked away that time he was more than confident that I would not only give him a good match but that I would make sure he looked good and strong.

Once we were in the ring, it was actually a simple match and of course I was there to do business, so I called what I thought was a pretty good match and put him over. As soon as I came back through the curtain, Terry Taylor was waiting on me. "Bobby, how do you do it?" "What?" "Get these big guys that are getting a push to take a bump for you. He went down about three times (actually he took two big bumps for me) and that was a good, good match."

"Was everything alright?" "Oh yeah, he was easy to work with, and no problems." I thanked Terry and waited for Brian to come back to the back. When he came through the curtain he shook my hand, thanked me big time and asked me if everything was alright. I told him it was a pleasure and hoped that he enjoyed the match. He said yeah and that it was actually one of the best matches he had had lately and thanked me again.

I left that day thinking I was glad I could work and I'm glad he had spoken with Dean about me, that way he could just relax and go out and get himself over. Plus, it was good to know that he did appreciate the match and I was treated with respect and he didn't just job me out or something. That was the last day of the tapings for me so I flew back home the next morning. I was scheduled to have the next week off until the following Monday. Well, as you know or will find out with me, one thing just leads to another.

On Tuesday of that week the office called me and wanted me to fly back out to do a, *Thursday Night Thunder* show which aired live on TBS. I'm really not sure which town or city I flew into, but I do recall that the show was in a big arena. I also remember that I had gotten to the arena earlier than usual due to the last minute flights they had booked me on. That's one thing about WCW, I couldn't tell you how many times, and I'm sure it happened to many others, they would just call me and I would have an eTicket waiting at the airport. Several of mine were so last minute the cost would be over two grand round trip, and I might have been returning to the same area I had just left. Yes, you read that right, I would be flying back into a city that I had just left. It was kind of crazy that way. Anyway, this was one of the times that I was happy to get called, because it was a chance to appear on live TV.

Let's fast forward to me getting to the town and inside of the arena. While I was sitting in an empty locker room, the building crew and staff and I'm sure many others were out in the building doing their thing. I mean this is a live event, and there's a ring being put together, TV set designs, and all the other stuff that needs to be done on the day of a big show. One of those things is a sound check. As I'm sitting there kind of in my own world I hear this voice. I know it, yet I don't. It's coming through loud and clear. The voice is booming..."Steve McMichael is the toughest player that I've ever coached." The voice kept saying stuff like "Let me tell you something about Steve McMichael..." and then the voice would put, "Mongo" over again. I must have just caught about the middle of it to the end, when it started again. "THIS IS COACH MIKE DITKA of The Chicago Bears. WINNERS of Super Bowl twenty..." The tape was on a continuous loop over and over again. The best way to describe it is like that scene out of *Apocalypse Now* when Martin Sheen's character, Captain Willard takes the surfboard from Robert Duvall's character, Lieutenant Colonel Bill Kilgore. Right after they leave the area, all you hear is the sound of those helicopters and Kilgore's voice booming, "I will not hurt or harm you. Just give me back the board, Lance. It was a good board... and I like it. You know how hard it is to find a board you like..." Well that's what it reminded me of. It was Coach Ditka's voice on a sound loop which was going to air later that night for Mongo when he was a part of "The Four Horsemen." I was sitting there getting chills listening to it over and over. It was part inspirational and part, "Don't mess with Mongo or somebody will get hurt," and I was fired up as I sat and listened. I had actually had a chance to work with McMichael a few months prior to this evening but he had opted out. That was the night I ended up having such a good match with Chris Benoit. After that match, McMichael came up to me and put me over by telling me what a good match I had. I told him I appreciated it as we shook hands. I never did get to work with him, but there was definitely some shared respect between us. Mine for my work rate, and his, well, you just don't play fourteen or fifteen years in the NFL as a defensive tackle or any position for that matter, and not be one tough SOB. He was the real deal.

Later on more and more of the boys made their way to the building and I went on over to catering to have a bite to eat. Most of the time, catering had some really enjoyable food, depending on the city and which company catered it. As soon as I entered I saw Brian sitting over at a table by himself. After I got my plate and drink I went over and asked him if it was alright if I ate with him. He told me sure, and asked me how I was. We made some small talk and I told him, "Thanks. I really appreciate what you did for me." "What?" I just looked at him, "You know, I know why I'm here and I appreciate it." Again, "I don't know what you're talking about." "Um, Okay, it's all good. Just know I'm glad to be here," I said. We finished eating and went our separate ways as we still had a few more hours before the matches were to start.

I knew that he must have sent word to the office and requested to work with me for his first live TV match since his arrival in WCW. We had just had that really good match on the previous Sunday and out of nowhere I get a call to come out to do a live event with him. It was pretty easy to figure out what was going on. I didn't mind. It was like getting another payoff, plus getting live television exposure is usually a good thing when you're with a big company and so many other people get lost in the shuffle. It also made me feel appreciated and respected by one of my peers as he trusted me enough to want me as his opponent in his debut. That's the education of a wrestler right there. It's when you know why you are there and what is expected of you once you get there.

A little later on, while I was getting ready for the match, he came up to me and wanted to know if it would be a problem if he didn't bump around for me like he had in the other match. I said it would be no problem whatsoever. I knew he had to look strong, so I knew it wasn't anything personal, it was business only. I asked him if he wanted the same match style or if he wanted to throw anything else into it. He said, "I'll let you call it, keep it about the same, except I won't go down on your comeback. I may or may not stagger back and hit the ropes or may no-sell it, we'll just go from there into the press and finish." Once we were in the ring it was all business. We had a really good match. He ended up dropping back off a couple of my kicks, but it still made him look strong. At the end, I think he threw in an extra kick or stomp. He had Virgil, who was the former bodyguard for "The Million Dollar Man" in the WWF, who was now working as, "Vincent" at ringside with him as part of the NWO gimmick. Once I was out from the finish and the kicks, Virgil did a little something to me for added effect, but both took good care of me and were very professional in doing so. Everything went well, and I was glad to do it.

Once I came back home the following day, it was just like another day at the office. I went to work. I got in a fight. Lost, and came home from work. But, the truth is, when I say it that way, that's just the way it was. There's a certain art to helping get someone else over, and I was good at it. This was one night I didn't kick out on two, but hey, you know what? *Pin Me Pay Me*, I'm good with that as well.

### ⤷ Back to the Indies ⤶

*Coming Up From the Indies*

Always remember that life isn't a destination it's a journey. I think Steven Tyler said something similar to this and got credit for it. I'm sure as talented as he is, he probably said many things and forgot he even said them, so I'll just use the quote here and give full credit to whoever wants to take it. I know, life's not a sprint, it's a marathon, or use whatever quirky life quote you want, and I do have a point to make here. For many in the wrestling business it's a long hard journey before you start making a dime or any real money in the business. It usually takes about seven years before a person really learns to work or get good enough to start making any real money. It's a hard business, that's just a fact.

I started off on the independent wrestling circuits around the Kentucky area before going down to Tampa town, where I received more training, and still continued to work on the independent circuit. Early on, there were many of these, "independent shows." Many "pro wrestling" shows started in circuses and carnivals anyway, and all might as well have been outlaws or independents or outside wrestling companies known as "outlaw shows." I guess nowadays

58

there are so many independent shows out there there's too many to count. I'm not here giving you a history lesson anyway, just look online and see how many "wrestling companies" there are and then look and see how many of the websites refer you to the WWE web site for references. Total bullshit, but they just build their data right along with whatever they think you will buy into or are gullible enough to swallow. So anyway, other than the protection I'm about to mention, outlaw and independent groups are and always have been about the same. Basically, if your wrestling company wasn't a part of the NWA, and even the WWWF was a part of it, you were known as running, "outlaw shows."

I guess it's the same as independent wrestling, but back then the NWA at least would come in and help protect you or your town from these outlaw shows popping up here and there trying to hustle people out of their money by "promoting" shows by using guys with names that sounded similar to the real professionals of the day. Some did

*Blaze with Lord Zoltan, Ken Jugan*

run legitimate shows as opposed to just ripping people off. Anyway, at some point anyone who didn't work for a bigger territory like out in Texas, or in Florida, the AWA, the NWA, or the WWF, then you were an outlaw promotion or an independent company or independent wrestler. Fact is, even today, even if you have a WWE contract, you're still just an independent contractor. Anyway, you can look up the facts and learn more about all of this if you want, but the bottom line is, nowadays if you don't work for a company that has a big name or has a big TV deal, then you're considered an independent or indie guy who works on the indie circuit.

Guess what, that's where most guys start and that's where most guys finish out their careers. I never minded working on the indie circuit because I could work for who I wanted and work when I wanted. The money issue is a completely different story when it comes to working for indie shows rather than big shows, but there is money to be made out there if you're willing to put in the effort to stay booked as regularly as possible. I personally made as little as ten dollars for two different matches when I first started, both thankfully were rather close to where I was staying each time and I had traveled with a couple other guys, so ten dollars is ten dollars. I then started making twenty-five dollars on a regular basis and soon that went to fifty. Now this isn't some overnight success story or secret, I'm just talking about how it was for my career.

The first full time contract I signed was for five hundred dollars per week but I was working seven days a week and many times twice on Sundays doing double shots. After about three weeks that went to six hundred dollars a week. That wasn't bad for someone training, traveling, and wrestling all the while gaining valuable lessons about the business. I even did a few WWF shows and made three fifty for a couple of shots and one time I did a three day run with them and made over seven hundred dollars. That wasn't bad money for a couple of days' work. Now, as many know, I hate the word, "jobbing" as I feel we all have a job to do in the world. But going on national and international television and putting over mainstream wrestling superstars and getting paid to do so, call me, or it, what you will. The thing I never could figure out was why the only ones bitching or who ever said something about doing a TV job were guys who were never in the business, saying they saw you on TV, or guys that were so called "workers" who were never good enough to be invited to come up WCW or WWF/E to do a job. They were the same guys saying, "Hey Bobby, look at me I have a replica belt and wrestle in front of 42 people once a month. I would never go on TV and get beat like that." Well no shit Sherlock! You were never good enough!

I have been with the same bank since 1986 and I have been through three different loan officers, the latest one has been my banker for over twelve years and is retiring after being in the banking business for over forty years. Guess what, he's a wrestling fan, and never once did he ask me if I won or lost my match. He just made sure my house or car payments were on time. There were many times we did talk about wrestling and how I was doing, but he never said, "I saw your win the other night or I heard you lost on TV the other evening." He could care less if I had won or lost. He was interested in me as a person and as a customer at his bank. He's a businessman. That's all you are as an independent wrestler as well, an independent business man.

At one point I was basically making a grand per match while working for WCW. Now that might seem like a lot of money, and it is, but you also have more expenses as you're on the road traveling more and more to make more and more. It can be a vicious cycle. Of course I would gladly take a grand now for a match, but I'm not taking any bumps, putting anyone over, and I have to travel first class. I kid, I kid. But my point is you can be making this kind of money with a big company versus the money difference being made working on the indie scene. I think you have to be happy with what you're doing in your job. WCW gave me many opportunities, but that was also a time when even though I loved being there, there were many times that, even though the money was great, it didn't make me happy. The old saying that "money can't buy happiness" held true for me, when I felt like, at times, I wasn't being used "to the best of my abilities," that's when I felt none too happy, but it paid the bills. Having been involved in wrestling for most of my adult life and a lifelong fan, I loved the fact that I actually had a chance to, in reality, make good money doing something I loved doing. But with some of the backroom politicians doing their thing and lots of other talented guys there, at times it was a miserable place to be.

But, you try to stay happy and realize that you are providing for your family and, to back up what I said about going and doing jobs for the WWF at the time years earlier, why not? You mean you're going to pay me to drive or fly all over the country, provide me with backstage catering with many times, excellent food, and then pay me, give me actual money to do something I love doing? Um, sure, let me think about it for two seconds, yes, book me, or yes, I'll take that booking. But, to the guy who can do a back flip and call himself a wrestler and who wants to stay home with his replica title belt, rather than work a match fifty to five hundred miles from home, because he would rather go over than put over a great wrestler, I get it. I can see where you would prefer to take your so called title so serious, and make twenty dollars to go over rather than make one hundred and fifty dollars and gain national exposure, that you'd rather pretend you're a "champion" than put another champion over. Sarcasm intended! You wanted to be happy. No, you're an idiot who never got or understood this business and never will.

Now, on the tail end of my run with WCW, when I went back to working the indie scene again, I enjoyed it just as much. The writing was on the wall in WCW. The WWF did call me, and we just never came to an agreement over a couple of minor details, and that's a shoot. Looking back, I probably should have gone to at least a couple of their TV tapings, but I had other plans. I even talked about coming into ECW, but again, it seems every time I called they didn't have anything for me, so who knows what could have happened, but it didn't matter, things turned out the way they should have, and I was back on the indie scene, working... Sure I enjoyed the money/payoffs, especially in WCW but I wasn't happy just because my check came. I was more concerned about doing my job than having a job. When my contract wasn't picked back up, I wasn't surprised per se. I knew that I could go back to Japan to make money, as I had left there on good terms. Plus I knew I could return to any number of smaller companies, where I still could get a decent night's pay. I also knew I could now charge a little more for my nightly fee because I was fresh from the national TV exposure of WCW. I would be used in the right way on these shows and I could once again feel good about what I was doing in the ring. This also gave me more control over what my schedule would be like and how much I would travel and how far I would travel. I was happier with less money, but with more freedom. The fact was I was more in control and loved being utilized to the fullest extent of my abilities, and I loved it. The money pays the bills, and sometimes you have to take a side job or second job or two, but that's alright, because at that time I still got to wrestle, and that is what made me happy. Remember, "It's not how much money you make, it's how much you save."

## ❧ Cleveland Rocks ❧

Looking back on my many memories of working on the indie scene in professional wrestling it's probably easiest to sum most of it up in this story about working or wrestling in Cleveland, Ohio. It could have been any town or city and with any number of different guys. Cleveland just happens to be a place I worked in a lot through the years and I think it's a pretty cool place. I've been to a lot of cool places and got to hang with some cool people. Lucky for me, most of the towns and cities that I had the opprtunity to work in regularly had some cool guys to work with and hang out with. Here's just a sample of some of the kind of crazy things that can and do happen when you're on the road wrestling on a regular basis. I don't want to leave out anyone or any town out but really the only things that change are the names.

The first time I went to wrestle in Cleveland, Ohio it was for Cleveland All-Pro Wrestling. It was a three day loop that should have been called the, "Titty Bars and Big Cigars Tour." Well, maybe not, but I did spend a lot of time after the matches hanging with a good group of guys and some new friends including a group of people who I would rather forget hanging out with during one Saturday afternoon. I'll tell you more on that in a bit.

The first time that I went there, JT Lightning had booked me along with Jimmy Valiant, Super Mario, and, "The Raging Bull," Manny Fernandez. Manny is one of the most legit tough guys that I have ever met in the wrestling business. That's a shoot! We ended up becoming fast friends and ended up working on many future shows together.

JT had started CAPW from this first set of three day shows and kept it running up until his death. He was so respectable of the wrestling business and he tried to run the best professional wrestling shows possible. He ran some of the best indie wrestling shows that I was ever on. In addition to using some veterans on those first few shows he booked

63

future WCW star, Johnny Swinger, and future WWE stars Edge and Christian. You could tell that they all were going to be future stars, as there was just something about all three that set them apart from new guys breaking into the wrestling business. Through the years JT would end up booking all kinds of future stars such as Austin Aries, Kazarian, and future WWE Champion, CM Punk. JT also booked many others who would one day become impact players in pro wrestling. I remember meeting Ryhno on a few shows there, and to me Terry is one class act. His talents have kept him in a job in all the major companies in the US as well as around the world. JT also helped develop and break in his regular crew who were all good workers as well, guys such as, Jason Bane, Sheiky Baby, Iron Man Nick, and Big Josh, "The Canadian Bad Boy." I remember other young up and coming stars coming in from Michigan like "The Amazing N8," "The Motor City Machine Guns," Chris Sabin and Alex Shelley and really just too many others to list.

My good friend JT Lightning & me in CAPW

CAPW had all these talented young guys come from Detroit, Chicago, and all around just to get the experience, and many went on to flourish in the business. If I left you off the list, my bad, but suffice it to say there were a lot of guys who I met through the years when I used to work on the indie scene.

My travels to Cleveland were always filled with fun nights after the shows. Of course as I said, I could say this about many other towns such as Knoxville, Tennessee, Pikeville, Kentucky, and Pittsburgh, Pennsylvania. You could always count on some kind of wild happenings around these towns after the matches. I met many good people through the years while I was in wrestling, again, the people I meet. I mentioned earlier, while working for CAPW, I used to pick Tommy "Wildfire" Rich up at the airport on a Thursday or Friday and travel with him while we did a three or four day loop around the Cleveland area. Of course our first stop would always be at a local package goods store for a case of beer and we would end up with us splitting a hotel room for the weekend. See, I told you in the last story I would mention it again. "Somebody say something 'bout cold beer and fried chicken?" I can hear "Wild Fire" now still saying that on many a road trips.

It was also on my first trip that I met Bo Barns. We just hit it off from the first night that we met. We laugh about being "bothers from different mothers" as we used to have a laugh or two about a few other things we indulged in through the years. Strip clubs weren't really my thing, but I do like me some strippers. They are actually a lot like the boys in that they are just "working" to make or earn their money. I have paid for many young single moms' education through the years, as they all seemed to be, "Just working my way through college," ha-ha, or so I have been told. You'll read more on this elsewhere in the book.

Back to that first night, Bo bought a case of beer and if I recall, even though we did visit the local strip club, we spent most of the night in the room partying, just laughing and having a fun time. The other funny thing that I recall about my first loop there was on the first night when Bo brought some guy who had eaten a bunch of "magical mushrooms" to the show. This guy looked like Lance, the surfer guy from, *Apocalypse Now*. It was hilarious watching this guy in the crowd, tripping as he had his face painted, no shirt on, and screaming and cheering like he was at a *WrestleMania*.

One of the funniest things to ever happen to me on the road also took place in the city that rocks. It actually happened right down by "The Rock-n-Roll Hall of Fame." My half-brother had traveled with me on the trip, and we ventured out to visit the HOF. We walked out on the pier area as we saw a bunch of other people doing on this sweltering hot July afternoon. My brother and I took our shirts off and just kept on walking with the crowd further and further into the crowd, and back towards the far end of this pier or pavilion area. Seeing how he was my half-brother and I had long bleached blonde hair and his head was clean shaven, we look nothing alike. The further we got back into the crowd, it seemed the more and more the others were "coming out" and doing some pretty heavy petting and

65

making out. The only thing about these couples who were making out was that they all seemed to be making out with members of the same sex. Hey, I'm open minded and probably the least judgmental person one could meet. To each his own is what I say, as long as it doesn't harm me or others. But this was getting a little too intense for me. I don't care who you love or who you marry, as that's your business, not mine, but this just wasn't my scene. It was also about this time that my brother kind of caught on to our surroundings, so we decided to do a 180 and high tail it out of this mass of "flamers and drippers." No offense intended but this was a different time period. No sooner had we turned around and started to head back toward the front area and out into the main streets, without even enough time to put our shirts back on, lo and behold, there's a TV camera pointed right at us recording the crowd. Without hesitating we just kept walking to get out of there without even thinking about why a television news crew was there. Let me tell you, we found out that night at eleven.

While in the motel room after the matches, drinking a few beers and getting ready to visit the local strip club, there it was. The lead in story that night on the local news was about how "The Gay and Lesbian Fundraiser Event" for an upcoming "Walk for AIDS" had taken place earlier that day downtown. And guess who was walking right there in the middle on the TV? That's right! It was yours truly and his half-brother. With wrestlers staying in rooms on either side of us, the walls started banging and you could hear all the other boys yelling all kind of unprintable things at myself and my brother. Bo just sat there looking at us, like, "What the hell?" But, it was all in good fun and we all soon got together in the lobby and had a good laugh before heading out for the evening. Looking back, I know this may not seem funny to some, and the fundraiser and walk were for a good cause, but it was one of those moments that you just had to be there to really appreciate it.

As I said, I always had a good time when JT booked me into the Cleveland area. I got to meet the great former NWA World Heavyweight Champion Harley Race on a show there. I had never met him, but had been a big fan of his for many years. I also got to work with all of the talent that CAPW had on its roster through the years as well as work with JT on many shows. On one loop, Ricky Morton, Sabu, and I had a six-man tag match with Tracy Smothers, "Dangerous" Doug Gilbert, and Tommy Rich. This turned out to be just a really good, good six-man tag match. I have to say that we "had them hanging from the rafters" that night. I had to add that line in there for Ricky, ha. Seriously, I later heard that there were a group of guys up in the WWE who were watching this match during catering and they were all enjoying some fine indie wrestling. That, to me is a compliment, when some of the other boys, especially guys who have made it up to "The Show" are watching guys who they knew were still working on a small show and doing their best to entertain fans. Yeah, I had some great times and wonderful memories from my many trips up to CAPW and working for JT. Like I mentioned, you could probably name ten other towns or cities that I enjoyed but, you know what? Cleveland Rocks!

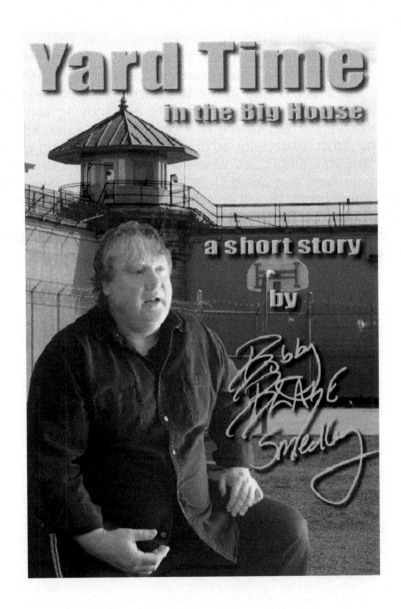

# Yard Time
## in the Big House

a short story

by

*Bobby BLAZE Smedley*

## ✧ Six ✧

## ✧ Yard Time ✧

*"Ask a group of school children what they want to be when they grow up and not one will say: 'I want to be a screw and look after tattooed psychopaths in a cold damp prison.'"—*
*Mark Chopper Read*

Prison, now there's a place to run a professional wrestling show. You already have a captive audience. I worked for the BOP: Federal Bureau of Prisons, which is a sub division of the U.S. Department of Justice, for almost two years as a corrections officer. As a CO I was responsible for the custody and care of federal inmates. The facility I worked at was called, Federal Correctional Institution Ashland, better known as "FCI Ashland." Prior to starting my job as a CO I had been doing some wrestling part-time and had just finished up working and training at Malenko's Professional Wrestling Academy in Tampa, Florida. The following story took place right before I signed my first full-time wrestling contract. While I was there, the prison would bring in all kinds of different types of activities, concerts, shows, and entertainers for the inmates. If you've never been to prison or don't know much about prison, let's just say it's an entirely different world. It's a world within itself. I had been going into this particular prison since I was 18 to play in a yearly basketball tournament they held there. I'm sure some of the guys there really enjoyed seeing a young long-haired blonde boy walking down the halls and out onto the basketball court. But, going back as a grown man, being an officer, and having been through the Federal Law Enforcement Training Academy gave me a little bit of a better perspective on things and I'm sure those inmates had a different opinion of me too. Hack, screw, a monkey with keys, hell, I've been called worse by wrestling fans, so this never bothered me much. The ones who used those terms were usually inmates and they didn't come right out and say it to your face. Now, the ones who call you "Boss" most of those guys are convicts. There's also a huge difference between fresh "fish" first timers, returning convicts, and "old timers." That's just a small insight into our penal system.

69

Anyway, trust me, when I say there's a difference between an inmate and a convict, I know what I'm talking about. I never had much trouble working inside the prison and a lot of it was because the BOP had good officers, and many of the convicts that I dealt with had a "Don't fuck with me, and I won't fuck with you" attitude. I can handle that. Hell, those guys had to live there. They were convicted felons who were stuck in prison. I could go home each night, they couldn't. I wasn't there to punish them, they were already being punished by being incarcerated, so I got along and did my time just like they did theirs, only I was on the right side of the fence.

One of the biggest attractions to ever walk through the gates of the prison while I worked there was none other than "The Greatest," Muhammad Ali. You may have heard of him. Not only is Ali still one of the most recognized sports figures in the world, he is one of the most recognizable men on the planet. Ali is widely respected and considered among the greatest heavyweights in boxing of all time. He was a huge draw not only in the world of boxing, but he drew people of every race, from every place throughout the world. You could feel the energy and excitement build as Ali made his way down the corridor and out onto the recreation yard, or as it's most often referred to, "The Yard." There are a lot of things that take place out on the yard. On this day Ali brought peace into a place that usually is full of violence. He gave the inmates an inspirational speech and finished it off by doing his famous "Ali Shuffle." This brought the inmates to their feet as they gave "The Greatest of All Time" a standing ovation.

In prison, inmates segregate themselves. They almost always stick with their own. That's just the way it is. White inmates only congregate with other whites, blacks with blacks, Hispanics with Hispanics, and Asians with other Asians. Many find safety in numbers. Many times non-racists turn racist in prison and again, it's not only to have a feeling of comfort in numbers, but also for protection. It's an entirely different world on the inside of a prison.

I point this out to emphasize the fact that when any type of entertainment was brought into the prison from the outside, generally only the inmates who were interested in that particular program would attend, many times based on race or ethnicity. For example when prison officials brought in rap groups, the blacks, and very few whites or maybe some others would go listen or watch. The same thing would happen if they brought in a country music act; mostly white, country, redneck, and maybe a few others would go watch. If a religious service or clergyman came in, and brought gospel music, well you get the picture. The list could go on and on as to what kind of entertainment could have been brought in, and each time the result was pretty much the same; that group or act catered to their direct demographic.

Ali transcended all demographics. He drew a crowd of people from every race and every type of inmate and convict in the prison. Well, guess what else transcends demographics? Professional Wrestling! People of all races and just about every ethnic group have some type of an interest in professional wrestling. Anyway, I was standing guard by one of the doors to a cell house as Ali walked down the hall.

There was already a huge buzz going on within the prison walls about his appearance. At the time I worked at this particular prison there were approximately 1,200 men incarcerated. Of the 1,200 or so men inside those walls, several were locked in segregation, while others had jobs that they had to attend to, such as in the kitchen, in order to remain on the strict schedule of events that take place on any given day on the inside. This left about 800 inmates who were eligible to go into the yard to see Ali. Not all did, but many did, and I'll get to that in a minute.

Several of the inmates, officers, and other staff members knew that I had been wrestling and that I had always wanted to pursue my dream of wrestling full time. I also knew several of the inmates in different cell blocks who tuned in weekly to any and all wrestling programming that was available at the time. So, I get the bright idea to approach the right people in each office from the physical director, the recreation director, the lieutenants, the captain and all the way up to the warden's office to get the approval and the funding to bring in a live professional wrestling event for the inmates. I couldn't believe it, but it got approved. A future date was set to have our very own live prison wrestling matches set up by yours truly, C.O. Smedley, aka Bobby

Blaze. Getting the show approved was the hard part as I had to go through the chain of command and also get the funding approved. The easy part was the advertising. It was the easiest advertising and the easiest event to promote. I'm not saying it was easy to pull off the actual event, but the advertising was at least easy. These guys see the same walls and same areas every single day. Stick a couple of posters in each cell block, a few more in the kitchen, and a couple in the gym and recreation areas, and every inmate would know that professional wrestling was going to be held inside of the prison. Plus word of mouth travels pretty fast in prison, believe that!

On the day of the event, everyone had to have a security clearance in order to get into the prison, plus we had to have a plan to get the ring into the prison and out into the rec yard. After all the proper checks and balances, clearances, etc. were completed, the ring had to be assembled. I owned the ring and I remember having it all loaded up on my dad's old red pickup truck. "Old Reliable" was a 1974 Dodge pickup truck with a homemade rack on top. I don't think dad ever intended to carry a professional wrestling ring around on it, but on this day he did. We only used one vehicle in order to speed up the entrance and exit process through the rear gate.

All the wrestlers had go through the front doors and clear the metal detector, go through two sally ports, and then pass through another set of iron gates before they could even enter into the long corridor where they would make their way out to the rec yard. Everyone involved on the show had to be there by noon. Everyone also had to have a special stamp on their wrist that could only be seen under an ultraviolet light. Everyone had to hope their stamp still was visible when the time came to exit the prison facility. The ring truck was cleared first and then word came for the officers to bring the wrestlers on through the gates and into the prison. All of this was done under the escort of correction officers who remained with them at all times.

Once the truck was out on the rec yard, inmates who either worked in the recreation department or others who had volunteered had that ring set up in record time. The show was allotted a two hour time frame which was to include the putting up of and the taking down of the ring, plus the five-match card that I booked. The actual show was to take place between one o'clock and three o'clock. The ring was set up out in the middle of a couple of full court basketball courts, and bleachers were pulled in on all four sides. I had done a little homework, plus, as anyone who knows about running a show, everyone who thinks they know about wrestling wants to be a part of the show in some way. Well believe it or not, there was a guy who was locked up who had done some wrestling announcing in his days on the outside. He had worked for the NWA back in the day. He had several pictures of himself on set with several of the boys, so I knew he was legit about it. There were a couple of guys who had been disc jockeys on the outside and they agreed to do the announcing. There was a guy who had boxed professionally out of Louisville who had worked with some of the top heavyweights back in his younger years, and again, he had proof as he had some photos and an old Kentucky boxing license mailed into him so he could show me. It wasn't that I didn't want to believe these guys, but they were convicted felons. It makes one wonder how all these honest men got sent to prison? They were all innocent.

That is they were all innocent except the one man who was such a die-hard wrestling fan that he wanted to be my manager on the day of the show, "You know, just to make sure you win." In his words, "I did it Boss. When they caught me, I had a new Cadillac, a trunk full of coke, a wad of money, and a couple of guns." That's the making of a good manager right there. This guy was about fifty at the time and he had been a lifelong wrestling fan. He was a huge fan of the old NWA and was a big fan of the Bill Watts UWF territory, as he was from Oklahoma. Without smartening him up, I told him that he could be my manager in the main event. Hey, I worked there, and I booked the show, who do you think is working the main event?

The show took place on a Sunday afternoon on a cool but sunny October day. The inmates started gathering and hanging out around the rec yard as soon as it was unlocked. Some started hitting the weights, others did their daily laps around the track, but most of them were busy segregating themselves into the four sections of bleachers that had been

73

set up. Again, blacks sat with blacks, Hispanics sat with other Hispanics, the white guys started sitting with other whites. It was like I mentioned earlier in the story.

Except, in each of these large groups of men they further segregated themselves. The DC blacks wouldn't sit near the Miami blacks, even though they were all seated in the same bleacher area. The biker white boys, or pecker woods, sat with other biker types, but nowhere real close to the other white guys. The Mexicans were with other Mexicans, but not seated close to the Colombians or other Hispanic prisoners. As those three sides filled up rather quickly, the other section of bleachers had all the leftover guys sitting around to watch the show. These were guys that weren't associated with gangs, no matter their race. These were guys that were outcast within the prison such as pedophiles, snitches, and bitches. Yes, even in prison there are many unwanted sickos, and child molesters are at the top of the outcast list. Nonetheless, those metal bleachers were filling up quickly too with an imprisoned audience of wrestling fans.

Once again, about 800 of the approximately 1,200 inmates were eligible to make it out to the rec yard to see the live wrestling. I make mention of this because I knew how many of the 800 inmates had been present when Ali had made his appearance. I also knew that like Ali, professional wrestling crossed over racial boundaries and religious affiliations, and would be a highly entertaining sporting event for these incarcerated men. Ali had drawn 667 inmates out on that same rec yard when he spoke to the men and did his shuffle. On the day that I brought pro wrestling inside those gates, we drew 661 drug dealers, murderers, bikers, rapists, hoods, thugs, and other rude, crude, and sociably unacceptable inmates and convicts who just wanted to feel normal and watch some good old professional wrestling. On this day, they were a million miles away from being incarcerated. They were just a bunch of men that were hanging out within their own little social, or not so social, group of friends and acquaintances getting ready for a day at the matches. I think it made them feel like men again, and if not like men, at least human beings.

Drawing this many people made me feel good on several levels that day. One, as a professional wrestler because I knew wrestling would draw. I knew those men would appreciate a good show. Two, and more importantly to me, as a man and a human being, I knew those guys wanted to feel normal for a couple hours rather than like caged animals. Those guys may have all been convicted and proven guilty of some unspeakable crimes, but they were still human beings. I also knew that no matter what they had done on the outside, on this day, they were just a bunch of guys wanting to watch some professional wrestling, like men.

With a one o'clock bell time and a ring surrounded by a bunch of loud and rowdy convicts it was show time. As I mentioned, I had tried to involve as many inmates as I could into the show in some capacity. The two guys, one black and one white who had said they'd been disc jockeys on the outside took turns announcing each opponent. One would announce the heel, the other the baby face, and that was cool. They actually played music and told a few jokes in between the matches so that worked out well as part of the show. Both men did a very professional job actually. I used the former ring announcer to announce each man from the center of the ring, after both had been introduced coming into it. He did a spot on very professional job. I even let one guy referee a match without smartening him up much other than telling him to, what else but, "Call it like you don't see it ref." He had to live there, so he didn't see much when it came the heels cheating and getting their heat. I seem to recall that all the heels got the biggest pops and cheers during the matches while the baby faces, myself included, got booed. Imagine that. Bad guys cheering for the bad guys!

Bell Time! One o'clock on the nose. We had to start right on time and we had to time everything precisely to be completely finished up and back out of the gates before the four o'clock "standing count." The standing count is one of five daily scheduled counts. When "Count time! Count time!" is announced out loud every day, no matter where you are in the prison, you have to be standing. The standing count would be followed by chow time, so it was extremely important for us to be out of that prison by four. As I mentioned, our allotted time when the actual show was to take place was from one o'clock until three o'clock. We had to have the ring truck and all of the wrestlers off the yard and out of the prison by three–thirty sharp.

Music played and the first two wrestlers hit the ring to a loud roar of applause. There was the clapping of hands, foot stomping, and cheers from everyone. Everyone seemed to be having a blast already and the two grapplers hadn't even locked up yet.

One of the funniest things that took place was when the referee went to check each opponent's boots, knee pads, and hands etc. per what a ref usually does prior to every match. An inmate stood up and yelled, "Give him a cavity search!" Loud boisterous laughter ensued throughout. I can assure you that in prison; a cavity search is not when a dentist looks into your mouth for cavities. In prison, a cavity search is a little more detailed. Let's just say every orifice is involved, including having a guard playing proctologist when these searches are performed. Every inmate could relate, as all had to have had one if not many during their time in the big house. So, the comment, as well as the loud laughter, was well justified. Good comedic timing as well by the inmate who yelled it. A cavity search, Ha!

Match one had a typical baby face going against a mysterious "masked man" from "parts unknown." On this day the mystery man was my brother Jimm working as, "The Scorpion." Going under a hood inside of a prison automatically gets you over as a heel. He got the huge response we were hoping for to open the show. Other than a few of the inmates yelling for the baby face to, "Take his mask off! Take his mask off!" he was mostly over with everyone because he was the heel.

Now, the funny thing was, beginning in this match and all the way through the main event, and I won't make mention of every match, but what was so comical was, an old white guy, started yelling in this match, and I mean yelled it throughout every match, "Drop kick that motherfucker!" He must have yelled, "Drop Kick" add your own explicit word here at least once every three to five minutes in every match. It may have started with MF'r, but he added some real colorful words, "Drop kick him in the nuts," and other things are usually only heard in a prison environment or friendly local grade school nowadays. The

Scorpion, being the worker he was, had a pretty good drop kick if I do say so myself. And I do say so. So he threw in a drop kick as a heel, and it went over well. I think he did it hoping to please and shut up the old timer. It didn't! One drop kick wasn't going to shut this guy up now, or in any match. It must have been the only wrestling move the guy knew. It was actually pretty funny because it was almost like he timed it throughout the rest of the day, so that when everyone was watching, and it would quiet down just a little, he would shout it out again. So, anyway, back in the ring, it was a quick roll up with the feet on the ropes and while holding his opponent's tights just for good measure, the Scorpion won the match much to the delight of the rabid heel crowd.

The next three matches all got over well with everyone. The show was coming off without one glitch. Music played in between matches, inmates cheered, talked, danced, some took a few little smoke breaks here and there, but almost every one of them sat there clapping and stomping their feet on the metal bleachers having an extraordinary time, considering they were incarcerated. The only complaint that was heard, and this was usually followed by brassy laughter was, "We wanna to see some women wrestlers! Where's the girls' matches?" There was no way I could have booked any female wrestlers on this show, and if I had, we would have had a riot on our hands for sure.

When it was time for the main event to take place this big, gruff, 300 pound bearded tattooed biker looking guy came out and grabbed the microphone. The inmates all got quiet. It had been going well, but it was about to get a hell of a lot better. Usually when it's quiet in a prison there's trouble brewing somewhere or something is about to go down. The yard is a place where a lot of action goes down in a prison. At the drop of a hat the shit can and will hit the fan. These guys are ready to rock and roll at any given time and many have nothing to lose if it does go down. Thankfully that wasn't the case. They wanted to hear what this guy had to say about his opponent, me, an officer who worked there. For the most part inmates hate screws, and I was no exception during this time.

Now, keep in mind, I was supposed to be the baby face, yet I had a heel for a manager, and was a heel for being a CO, and for being a baby face. Double heat instantly! I had privately told the little old short guy who wanted to manage me to wait out by the announcers' table. I told him to not do anything until he saw me coming out. He did exactly as he was told, in fact he stood right there the entire show until I came out. This was when things were still pretty much kayfabed, and I for one, wanted this show to be kayfabed as much as possible for the inmates. They weren't dummies just because they got caught committing a crime, some were smart guys, but, as I said, they just got caught. I wanted these guys to feel like humans, and like men again, even if it was just for a few brief hours. So, that's why I had told the old die hard convicted fan to wait until I came out before I would see him and then, and only then, he could escort me to the ring.

The ref was in the ring. The two disc jockeys who had been MC'ing the event had no clue, and in fact, I had no idea what was going to happen other than I knew the finish. Once, "The Outlaw" grabbed the mic, all three men backed away. I don't think anyone knew what he was gonna say or what was gonna happen. I know I didn't.

"I understand that this Bobby Blaze is a CO here this fine institution. It's a damn shame that they keep innocent men such as yourselves locked up. I know, the COs know, and even the warden knows that each and every one of you are innocent. You're all a bunch of good guys, just like myself. Well, I'm gonna do all you inmates a favor today. Bobby Blaze won't be back to work in this slammer for a while because in just a few minutes, I'm gonna break his back!" HUGE POP! You talk about getting over with a bunch of condemned, convicted men. The Outlaw's promo brought a thunderous roar that hadn't been heard that loud since Ali had done his world famous shuffle out in that same rec yard a few months earlier.

I didn't even wait for the music to start, I just knew it was time for me to hit the ring and get on this big bastard. I would have to save some face with these guys. I had to work there. I needed to work stiff, fast, and hard. I needed to get over no matter what. I knew, even though I was the face,

78

and he was the heel, that shit just got real in here, and I would be the one getting real heat if I didn't fight and make this match look like an absolute shoot. That wasn't the plan before the promo. The plan was, I would work as a baby face, The Outlaw would work as a heel, and we would try to have the best match possible and to make it, since it was the main event, the best match on the card. That was the plan. Little did we know what was going to happen during the match especially after the improvised promo.

I charged into the ring and we started at it hard. We went back and forth with stiff forearms and kicks before we took it outside the ring and fought our way around all four sides of the ring, going back and forth with kicks and punches. We finally got back into the ring and forcefully pushed away from each other, making sure that the ref knew to try to retain some order or it was gonna get too far out of hand. The little manager ran around the ring cheering me on and I think he, like the ref, actually thought we were gonna kill each other before this thing got settled down. There is no way to describe what happened next. Call it divine intervention or whatever you want, but to this day I still have no answer as to what happened. Not one wrestling move had taken place during our brawl, but as soon as we locked up in the middle of the ring, The Outlaw picked me up to suplex me. He held me in a vertical suplex position for about seven or eight seconds before dropping us both down, dead center in the middle of the ring. When he did, one of the side rails snapped and the entire ring collapsed. We both went straight down through the plywood and the wooden slats under the ring and straight down into the asphalt of the basketball court the ring was centered on.

BOOM!

The ref went down too. The little manager was outside the ring, and all I remember was him grabbing and pulling my leg to help me get out from underneath the canvas, busted wood, and twisted metal. He was asking something about whether I was alright. There's no booker alive who could have called that finish or booked that show any better. The problem was, it wasn't booked that way and it wasn't the "planned" finish. Divine intervention? Luck? I have no idea.

I heard The Outlaw moaning, "Pin Me," but it was all I could do to get out from under that mess. Two of the ring posts were bent inwards and two were still relatively intact and upright. The prisoners were going crazy! They thought that this had been a part of the show. I knew different. I slowly climbed out of the broken ring, climbed up onto the top of one of the ring posts, and even though I knew I was gonna basically be landing on concrete or asphalt, I had to pin this man. He couldn't even get up. I had to do it. I did my best, that's right, "drop kick that motherfucker" ever and landed down on top of the prone, barely moving Outlaw. The ref reached around from his back and counted three and believe it or not, the place popped again. The prisoners were going crazy! Honestly, I could barely stand up at the time, and The Outlaw could hardly do anything but continue to lie there. I made my way back out to the ground where my manager raised my hand like I had just defeated King Kong. Again, all the inmates stood, applauded, whistled, clapped, and raised all sorts of hell as they had just witnessed one fine professional wrestling show and one helluva pro wrestling match.

Many of the guys came over and thanked me for bringing the show into the prison. Some thanked me while others congratulated me on the match. The ring guys who had helped assemble the ring started loading everything back into the truck as the announcement was made that rec time was over and inmates should return to their units. It was three o'clock. Perfect! We had thirty minutes to get the ring truck off the yard and the boys back out of the front gate before that standing count. The ring crew, with the assistance of the inmates who worked in the rec department pulled double duty to make sure we could make the clearance. I went to the back of the rec office and thanked the guys for working so hard on the show and to just sit tight until we were cleared to exit the building, which would happen after the ring truck was cleared to exit the rear double sally port, through another set of double fences with razor wire on the top. There also had to be a perimeter security truck at each entrance before anyone could leave. The buzz of loud laughter and excitement could be heard throughout the rec yard as the inmates were filing back out from the yard into the unit area where they would have to get ready for that four o'clock standing count. But, for the last couple of hours of their life, I know one thing, they felt like men again. They had just had one of the best times of their incarcerated lives. Through my professional wrestling, I know, on this day, I made some guys feel not only like men again, but maybe even made them feel like human beings again. Now that's a good finish.

## ✄ Seven ✄

*"The greatest hold in professional wrestling is the hold it has on its fans."*

## ✄ Either by a Pin Fall or a Submission ✄

*Great holds and moves in professional wrestling*

There are so many different holds and moves in wrestling it would be hard to count each and every one of them. I'm sure there's a list somewhere, but I bet that it's not even complete. There have been books and DVD's that demonstrate many of the ones used in everything from amateur wrestling to legitimate shoot fighting. I just thought it would be fun and somewhat educational to give my insights into some of the different holds and moves that have been used in pro wrestling. Please keep in mind, many of these very holds can be used in a real fight situation. If you were to front face lock someone or chicken wing a person on the street, it doesn't take much to put a guy out pretty quick. Trust me when I tell you that, it can and has been done, more than once. With that said some of them are dangerous, so don't try this at home kiddies. First, let me state that there is a difference between wrestling holds and wrestling moves. Again, I'll be talking about the ones used in the pro style that you watch on TV. Oh, before I forget, don't bother looking for my list on the internet because almost every site takes you to some WWE sponsored site that only gives the names of the ones that their wrestlers use. Folks, this isn't a knock on the WWE, but it just shows the power that they have when it comes to marketing and also trying to make everyone believe that they, The WWE or their performers actually came up with a particular hold or move. Now, a hold is something that you get your opponent in, and well, hold them there or immobilize them. The moves, and I'm not talking, "high spots" for all you little spot monkeys out there who think I'm out of touch with today's product, I'm talking moves that are actually executed on your opponent during the course of the match.

In no particular order, the first one that comes to mind is one that seems like it used to be everyone's favorite hold when I was growing up, "The Sleeper Hold." You remember it too. Everyone seemed fascinated by the dreaded sleeper hold. The sleeper hold actually does work if properly applied as I can attest to as witnessed back in junior high school when Mr. Howell put it on Dave Johnson one day. Mr. Howell was a big burly man who had fought in WWII. One day while Dave was joking around with him Mr. Howell kindly showed Dave just how effective the sleeper hold could be. After a few good laughs, we knew then and there that when we watched professional wrestling each Saturday morning that if someone put the sleeper on their opponent, it's was lights out. The Sleeper!

The next hold that comes to mind is, "The Boston Crab." At one point or another when young boys wrestle around and horse play one of the two used to get the other in this hold. I'm not sure if it was because it was easy to do to another person or just because we had seen it on TV. Either way it seems everyone has been in or put the Boston Crab on someone. I know Chris Candido used to love to get me in this hold. Each week on TV, I would sell, sell, sell, and eventually after several weeks, I would make it to the ropes. It made for a rest spot for our high impact and high energy matches. I used to be so flexible I didn't mind it done to me when applied properly, but now, and of course, I am older and due to a lack of flexibility in my back, I say no thanks. Take it from someone with a bad back, if someone applies this hold on you, tap out! The Boston Crab!

Watch out for, "The Abdominal Stretch." "Oh my God Bobby he's ripping my insides out. He is killing me! My God Bobby, please. Check the ropes; I think he is going to kill me. I think my insides are coming out, my intestines, my God, he is ripping me in half." I was trying hard not to laugh or break character as these were the words of Louie Astria one night as Rico Frederico applied the abdominal stretch on him. I was refereeing some matches in Ruskin, Florida back in the day, and Louie and Rico were the main event. Louie had me in stitches as he was selling this hold during the match. Of course, being the ref there were certain things I wasn't supposed to see, like when Rico would use the leverage from grabbing the ropes to stretch Louie even more. I almost couldn't keep a straight face the entire time. I think I was more entertained than the fans on this given night or at least during this match. I was living with my brother Jimm at the time and couldn't wait to get home to tell him about how Louie was selling the abdominal stretch. We still talk about it to this day. The Abdominal Stretch!

So, how about the "Camel Clutch?" Maybe you know it as the Steiner Recliner, I know I do as I've been in it and it's no fun. But, think about the voice of The Iron Sheik saying, "I win the Dubya Dubya F World Title with my Camel Clutch. I break the Hulk Hogan back. That jabroni no champion. Iron Sheik real world champion." Yep, The Camel Clutch is the real deal if a man can win a world title with it, so it must be real. Besides that, according to Sheiky Baby, he will humble you if he gets you in it. The Camel Clutch!

Finally for the last hold I'll mention before moving on to moves is, "The Figure Four Leg Lock." When guys are working, the above mentioned holds can be easily applied, if one knows what they are doing. I'm not saying the average Joe can put these holds on you, but if a guy knows what he's doing he can snatch you up or take you down and get you into one of them pretty quick. Some can even be grabbed and applied once you have someone in the right position in a street fight. The figure four takes a little bit more effort and is harder to actually put on someone without them helping or cooperating just a little bit, nonetheless, it's legit. Don't let your friend talk you into letting him get you in the figure four. Serious damage can result! On the plus side, if you're the one putting it on someone else, the end result could be sixteen world heavyweight titles. The Figure Four! "Wooooo!"

Like you, I can name a bunch more, but want to keep this light as I think everyone has their favorites. I can, but won't go into some of the more advanced holds. Many of them are the same, but have different names, but like my brother and I like to say, "Wasn't wrestling more fun when we were marks?"

Alright, moving right along into professional wrestling moves, here's a little list of some of my favorites. Please feel free to disagree with my list and have some fun with your friends and come up with you own list of holds and moves.

Have some fun with it when you do. Remember when pro wrestling was fun? I do! I always tell people when I autograph copies of my books, "Always remember the good memories that pro wrestling brought you." I'm very serious when I write that and tell you that now, because it's true. Think about all the fun that you have had by being a fan of professional wrestling.

First, and there's no way I'm leaving this move off my list is, "The Northern Lights Suplex." I fell in love with this move the first time I saw Dean Malenko execute it on TV for Sun Coast Pro Wrestling back when I was wrestling in The Sunshine State. I had ridden down to the show with him and was sitting ring side at the announcers table when he did it. Just like Cornette did years later when I first did this in SMW, I popped big time. I broke character and put it over. I had already worked earlier on the card as a heel and was out at the announcers table talking about issuing Dean a challenge during the next taping. After seeing him performing a Northern Lights Suplex I wasn't so sure. I knew then and there, I had to learn how to do it. All the way back from Sarasota to Tampa, I put it over in the car and bugged Dean to please show it to me during my next training session. It took months for me to learn as I always wanted to make sure I had a good arch in my back, that my neck was strong enough to absorb my weight, plus the weight of another man. I didn't want to mess it up once I learned it. I also wanted to make Dean proud that I could do it justice once I had his blessing to start using it. As I said, I didn't use it regularly until many months later when I finally got into SMW. The Northern Lights Suplex!

Next up, "The DDT!" Man that is one devastating move when done properly. I've had a couple of neck stingers from this one, and that was with me and another trained professional, and me doing my best to protect myself. Jake Roberts of course executed this move and made it famous throughout the world. When Jake hooked your head and neck in it, everyone in the building and those watching on TV knew it was lights out for his opponent. One mess up and you can do serious damage to a guy's head, neck, or both. There's a chance that even when the DDT is done properly one can be seriously injured. Remember when Jake did it to

Ricky Steamboat on a concrete floor? This is not a move to be taken lightly. Leave this one to the pros! The DDT!

Next we move on to, "The Power Bomb!" I call it, the dreaded power bomb. When it's done correctly and the one delivering it lays the guy out flat, it looks impressive. It's a highly effective wrestling move. If it's not done correctly, it can be disastrous. I know there are several variations of the power bomb nowadays, but we'll stick to just the regular or original variation. I'll add right here, I have had this move used on me and a guy didn't lay me out flat and I sincerely believe that was the beginning of most my neck damage. I was dropped about seven to eight feet right on the top of my neck and head and landed extra hard from not being laid out flat properly. If you're not familiar with this move, it's when one man, usually the bigger of the two, lifts another grown man up onto his shoulders with his back facing the mat. The person up in the air really has no idea when the impact is going to take place as he is slammed back first onto the mat. When you're up there, you really have no way of knowing how high up you are nor how close you are to hitting the mat until you are actually laid out on your back. That's the key, being laid out flat and landing flat. It just takes one fuck-up to do serious damage, as mentioned. I always tried to lay my opponent out flat whenever I did use a power bomb during a match. Yes, even when I did it to a wrestler named "Scab" I at least had the professional courtesy to lay him out flat. The Power Bomb!

One of my all-time favorite wrestling moves is, "The German Suplex." I think Karl Gotch was an early pioneer in doing, the German Suplex. If he wasn't the first to use it, he certainly was the first one who really perfected this move early on in professional wrestling. I'm not giving him all the credit as many others perfected it through the years, it was just that I first read about it and saw pictures of it being performed by Gotch way back when. Kurt Angle and more recently, Brock Lesnar and maybe a few others who had strong Olympic or amateur backgrounds all could snatch someone up and toss them back over their body making the German Suplex look so awesome. It's really more of a belly to back suplex, but when guys throw in that exquisite back arch, thrusting or popping their hips when they do, they really get the guy off the ground then lay him out flat; it's just a move of pure beauty. Again, the scary thing is when you're on the receiving end of one, you're not really sure when you're going to hit the mat because your head is facing away from the mat looking forward. The German Suplex!

Finally, the most devastating move in all of professional wrestling is..."The Pile Driver!" I personally think this is the most dangerous move in all of professional wrestling. It has been "outlawed" or "illegal" in almost every major territory or company through the years as every wrestling company needs that one move that is so vicious that, it's against the rules to do it on your opponent. I've taken it, and have had a couple of teeth chipped as well as neck stingers from receiving the horrific pile driver. The person receiving it is upside down, with his head between a guy's legs and his head is then driven down into the wrestling mat. Many guys have been legitimately injured from taking this move. You can look up and see or read about pile divers that have gone wrong and have either broken guys necks or at least put them out of action for months on end. It's probably my favorite move to see done on someone, but only if it's done correctly. The Undertaker and Kane still use what's called a Tombstone Pile Driver and I'm sure due to their size, athletic ability and experience they really protect their opponents when they perform their version of it. But the original pile driver, done properly only by a few is extremely dangerous. Way back when, and I'm talking years ago, Randy "The Macho Man" Savage did a pile driver on Ricky Morton through a table and it is to this day the most awesome pile driver I've ever seen. With that said, Savage wasn't known for using it, but there are a few guys who nobody can forget doing the pile driver. Harley Race used it to perfection. Of course everything Harley did looked like perfection in motion. Paul Orndoff did a jumping pile driver during his day and man did that thing looked like it either paralyzed or killed the guy when he did his. And, last but not least, Jerry "The King" Lawler had his pile driver. There are others through the years who used it, but Race, Orndoff, and Lawler all perfected it like no other. The most banned move in all of pro wrestling...The Pile Driver!

## ❧ Real Time ❧

## ❧ Fighting, Working, and Shooting ❧

### The Lion, the Lamb, and the Fox

I've been in many fights in my life. I'm not proud that I resorted to fighting, but am proud that I stood up for myself, or someone else, or for a just cause. There were times that I needed to survive. I might have fought to defend a friend, likewise a friend may have been there to have my back, or maybe it was to protect my brother. At times it was just because someone started some shit that they couldn't finish. I never took advantage of anyone. I never started one fight that I can recall, but I have finished many. I certainly let it be known that if you wanted to go, I was ready to go. Now I'm no bad ass, and don't claim to be. I'm just saying I have been in real fights, and also, fighting never really resolves anything.

If you recall my statement from my first book or if this is the first time you're reading or hearing this, listen up. Mussolini said, "It is better to live one day as a lion than 100 years as a sheep." I think I wrote it as, "It's better to be a lion for day than a lamb for a lifetime." But, why not be a fox? Sometimes it is wiser to just be a fox. There's truth in that. You need to stand up for yourself, and earn your rep as a lion, a fighter who won't back down or take crap off someone who wants to try to be a tough guy or run his mouth on you. Stand up for yourself! If you don't then you'll be a lamb or easy prey for the rest of your life. A lot of tough guys who I've met through the years were bullied early on, just like I was until one day you learn to fight back and people or these bullies leave you alone. The world is full of tough guys, most can be found in cemeteries. Now, I'm not writing this to encourage fighting, quite the opposite. So, keep these two things in mind, pain is temporary if you get in fight, but pride is forever, so stand up for yourself and your beliefs. And, two, yes, it's better to be a lion for a day than a lamb for a lifetime. But, rather than being a lion or a lamb, be a fox. A fox out thinks or out smarts them all. Choose your battles wisely. A fox knows when to simply walk away from the fight or altercation and come out much better off. Yes, I have a point to all of this. In the ring, we work; we try to make it look like a fight, hopefully without hurting each other too bad, but as the saying goes, "It's not ballet," it's supposed to be a fight. The fans know and have known for years what's going on to some extent, but they should see a live action contact, combat sport, or fight taking place in the ring. As for these fans, whether they are at the local high school or armory show, a huge event in a big well known arena, or just watching on television, they should be entertained. That's what they spent their hard earned cash to see, wrestling, but also, and more importantly nowadays, entertained. They should be surprised and not know everything, but just be a fan, watch a fight and be excited to be entertained. That's the working part of the fight. There should always be that blur between what's real and what's not. There's one thing it's not, and that is FAKE.

The blur! Yes, I do think there is a real blur between what is real and what is not real. There's a blur or fine line between making it look like you've hurt someone and actually hurting them. John Cena may have said it best, "I mean anyone who brings up the word 'fake' with me is truly ignorant of what we do. We entertain. We're TV that develops right in front of you as it happens. People think we are who they see. That's kind of true, but not. I mean, we're as real as fake can get. Like, I'm Superman, but I'm not. Although a lot of people in the business don't know when to turn the switch off, I do, and I'm John." "Hustle, Loyalty, Respect!" The words that Cena uses are a lot more than just a catch phrase. They are ideals to live up to, ideals that many in this generation of young wrestlers should try to live up to but many fall very short of. So the wrestler's job is to, fight and entertain, and the fan's job is to cheer, boo, get all excited, and guess what else? They should not only enjoy the show but they should be entertained.

Now that I've covered the fighting and the working, the difference of not always trying to be the tough guy by being the lion, or the weakling by being a lamb, let's talk about being a fox. Sure sometimes you have to fight in the real world. Celebrities, and I count the bigger stars in professional wrestling as celebrities, it seems can't go out anywhere nowadays without someone starting shit with them and then posting everything on social media. The entire world knows the moment that a pro wrestler is arrested, has been in a car wreck, has been injured, or been out and got into an altercation with a fan. And for the life of me, I can't understand why there's always some tough guy sitting at the bar who thinks that he can just whip a professional wrestlers ass when all he is doing is going out to have a cold beer, maybe relax with some friends or fans, and the last thing on his mind is wanting to fight some drunk asshole who thinks he's tough. Yet, it happens all the time. Through the years I've heard about some of the toughest guys in the business, guys like Meng, one legit bad ass, but a really nice gentleman, guys like the Barbarian, Harley Race, Dick Slater, and a bunch more guys who could just mop the floor with the average guy off the street. Even today, who in their rightful mind would want to go up to Brock Lesnar and start running their mouth, saying, "What you guys do is fake, and I bet you ain't so tough out of the ring," blah, blah, blah. Total ignorance!

Why? First off the wrestler has nothing to prove, he knows from being in professional wrestling, and from being a professional athlete, it's a no win situation for him, because A, he can get up at any time and just kick the shit out of the loud mouth, and B, more than likely every news outlet in the country will hear about it and it may even cost him his job, or at least a lawsuit.

So, here are a few of the ways I have handled some of these "shoot situations." I don't like to fight or want to, especially since I've aged a little, but I will if backed into a corner with no way out. First, I don't go out much, I know how bad my nerves are in crowds, and that causes me undue stress. Second, I don't go looking for trouble when I go out. I try to smile, make others feel at ease, but deep down, I put out the vibe of a "Don't fuck with me, and I won't fuck with you" kind of attitude. I have courage, and I won't back down, so I can be kind and smile at someone trying to be a tough guy, knowing that deep down, my fear is natural, but I can control it to my advantage. So when that boisterous arrogant loud mouth is yelling and trying to act all tough, I usually try to mind my own business, but if it's directed towards me or the people I happen to be with, I stand there and smile. I know deep down that that person deep down is either a bully or a coward. And, I know deep down that even if I have fear, deep down, I'm not afraid to fight, but deep down they will usually back down against a man who stands there, of course in a defensive position, but with a smile on his face. That's being the fox. I'm certainly not going to be their lamb. Yes, I'm willing to be the lion, but, what I'm really trying to do it is be the fox. That way, I can walk away without ever having to throw one punch.

Here are just a couple of things that have happened that I find funny. Most of these have been when I was out, many when I was younger, and the other person or persons were drunk or under the influence and they were the ones usually looking for trouble, not me. Some have happened more recently. Again, sometimes it's more fun being the fox.

A couple of guys were standing, well one was leaning up against a lamp post outside of a restaurant where a few of my buddies and I had just had watched some football on the big screen televisions over a couple of drinks and a nice meal. I walked out first with my best friend close behind, while the others remained inside talking to some other people, pissing, paying the tab, whatever. So, as I walk out and see these guys, and I make a quick read of them both, I know that they are probably up to no good.

They were probably looking for easy marks to beg money from, get smart with, or possibly follow people down the street harassing or intimidating them. The first guy standing there, says, "Hey, can I ask you a question?" I just looked at him dead serious and said, "I think you just did!" End of conversation. His friend or partner in crime just eased on back against the light post, and the guy who spoke moved closer to his friend, a few steps further from me and my friend, as we waited for the light to change so we could cross the street. I know, no tough guy move, but by reading the guy, knowing he was probably on drugs and was just going to try to bum money off me, I just shut him down quick.

My buddy just kind of laughed under his breath as we crossed over the street towards the car while waiting for our other friends to join us. It was just a matter of shutting the situation down quickly rather than engaging in some conversation which would have led to an altercation.

Another time, a guy was sitting at the end of the bar, being all loud, and basically annoying people by just being an obnoxious asshole, when the bartender mentioned to him, loud enough that I could hear it, "Hey see that guy over there? He used to be a professional wrestler and if you don't shut up or quiet down I'm gonna ask you to leave or have him kick your ass." Why bring me into this? He wasn't bothering me other than he was being loud. He hadn't said anything to me whatsoever. It was just a sports bar, and everyone was having a good time. I mean it wasn't some big bar that even had bouncers; it was just a hole in the wall sports bar that served hot food and cold beer, cheap. Anyway, I was there with a couple of my uncles, having a cold beer, again watching a football game, and minding my own business. So, the guy yells out cross the bar, "Hey you! Don't make me mad. You wouldn't like me when I'm mad." I just took a big gulp of beer, looked over at him, and said, "Make you mad? Hell, I don't like the way you are now, why would I make you mad?" A few people at the bar had a good laugh at his expense while I just kept looking straight at him until he looked away. He pretty much stayed quiet and to himself the rest of the game. He certainly didn't say anything to me. Again, there was no fighting; mere words were used, spoken with confidence, and out foxing someone. Of course, out foxing a drunk isn't that hard, but you get my point.

As mentioned, I've been in a fight or two, well, many, but I would rather not talk about, brag, or tell someone how tough I am. Sure, I was trained, and trained right. I learned to fight at an early age and through all of that, it only gave me more discipline. As stated, I never go looking for trouble and don't ever try starting a fight with anyone. I have confidence in who I am and what I know I can do. I know tough guys! Jails are full of tough guys and as I said, so are cemeteries. I'd rather not visit either one anytime soon as prison or death are not on my short list of things to do. These guys with big muscles, walking around in some Tap Out shirt, two sizes too small or some other MMA bullshit shirt on are easy to see from a mile away. They usually aren't the ones you have to worry about. They probably are just fans and have probably never been in a real street fight in their lives. Yes, there is a difference between being in a ring, be it, a boxing, wrestling, or octagon than being in a street fight. A street fight is a completely different matter. Now, that's not a dig, insult, or a challenge to anyone who wears that stuff or trains for boxing, wrestling, MMA or whatever their chosen discipline is. In fact, it's a compliment that these guys aren't the ones usually looking to start fights. If they are legitimately training for something it's usually called a discipline. It's called a discipline for a reason and it usually gives one discipline in more than just fighting, it gives them discipline in other areas of their life as well. So they more than likely aren't out looking for fights. If they are, well, then they are nothing but bullies who probably need a good ass whoppin' to set them straight, but I digress. It's usually the quiet ones, minding their own business, not looking for trouble that are usually the most dangerous ones anyway.

I'll give you a couple more examples about being a fox rather than trying to be a bad ass or a lion and not laying down like a lamb, but just a couple of stories to show you that fighting isn't always the answer to every problem in life. I just used good psychology and street smarts in both of these next two examples to avoid getting into a fight, or prison, or a cemetary.

Try to be cool to the bouncers. Some of these guys probably wanted to be in the business anyway, usually work out, and aren't looking to fight customers every evening anyway. I'm talking about some of your higher class clubs that have respectable doormen or bouncers who are trying to make a living, not the average guy who thinks he's tough at some shit hole in the wall bar where he works for free drinks. A couple of buddies of mine and I used to visit a certain club in Orlando. It was a high class strip club with some really hot dancers. They had two or three, depending on the night, biggest guys I had ever seen. These were just these big strong looking tough guys who you knew could and would fight if given the reason to throw someone out on their ass. By showing respect to them, they always showed respect back. They always got us tables up front, knew regular customers who would send us drinks and likewise we would send rounds of drinks to other regulars as well. Plus, we all knew and respected the girls. So if it's a nice club, be nice. If trouble does come your way, the bouncers are more than likely going to be escorting someone else out of the club, not you and your buddies because they know you probably didn't start it.

Once while attempting to sing karaoke, which I think can be fun, as I enjoy other people's talents, and sometimes, lack thereof. I fall into the lack of talent category when it comes to any type of singing. I have a voice others prefer not to hear when I try to sing. Anyway, there was a time when I used to at least attempt karaoke. Usually my friends would laugh at me as I tried to sing, but we always had a good time. I laughed along with them, hell I knew I couldn't sing. My friends, my family, and the boys, I'm sure would have preferred to not hear me even try to sing. Anyway, one night this wise guy gets smart, someone I don't even know, but he gets wise and starts cracking on me and I make a few jokes back to him still thinking it's all in good fun. Remember, I still had the microphone, and he was just trying to be loud and started to be a real prick. Right as I'm about to step down from the small stage, he stands up and says, "You better watch your back on your way home tonight!" I just smiled, looked right at him, and said, "I'm not going home; I'm going to your old ladies house tonight." Oh man, did he ever come unglued. All his friends or buddies even all started laughing at him at this point. He kept yelling and screaming crazy stuff like he was going to do something about it right then and there. Again, I just stayed calm and smiled, as I knew he was all talk. His buddies were trying to calm him down, but he was too blasted to realize he was just making more of a fool of himself with his idle threats. I just held my ground a few feet from him and in a non-threatening manner said, "I'm going out that door right there, and I'm going to my car. And guess what? I'm going home. Alone! Now, you can stay here and have a few more drinks and laughs with your friends or you can come on outside, that's up to you, either way, I'm going home." I had read him right, he was just a young, probably twenty-two or twenty-three year old college punk trying to show off to his school buddies or work mates. He even knew in his buzzed out mind that he was talking shit. He was all talk, and didn't stand a chance, especially since his buddies were laughing at him and telling him to just chill out and have a good time. I sure wish I knew where his girlfriend lived, because I sure would have gone over there and gave her something he must not have been, ha-ha. But, I didn't. I went on home without getting into an unnecessary fight.

Anyway there are fights, staged for entertainment purposes only to be enjoyed by you the fans, as it should be. There are legit bad ass guys out there who can work or shoot; again, in a work hopefully the shooter will work to entertain you the fans. And then there are tough guys who can shoot and really fight, and if they so desire, they will rip your spine out or at least fuck you up pretty bad. It's always best to avoid fighting. But if you must, always try to know when to be a lion, or a lamb, or to play the fox.

## ∾ The Iceman ∾

## ∾ Dean Malenko, The Man of 1,000 Holds ∾

Many people probably never realize just how good a worker and what a good shooter Dean Malenko truly was. I also probably didn't give him enough credit or emphasize just how much of an impact he had on my training and my wrestling career. He played a huge part in my early training. If Dean was, "The Man of 1,000 Holds" he probably taught me 999. The best one he ever taught me was my finishing move, "The Northern Lights Suplex." Okay, I know it's more of a move than a hold but you get my drift. I used to kid him that he probably actually knew a million and one holds and moves. He told me how they had let him use it in Japan, and taught me because I could do a good wrestling bridge. He encouraged me to give it try and see what happened. He said that it would be a great finishing move to use in the US as many people, even those in the business, hadn't even seen it yet. It took a lot of training for me to actually perform the move as smoothly as I eventually did. Not only did I work on it in the ring every chance I could, I also had the bright idea that I could benefit from using a thicker gymnastics mat and using a smaller person to practice or train on. I eventually perfected it using a kid I knew who was like in the 6th grade. He thought it was fun to get whipped over as the other kids looked on. I had it in the back of my mind before I finally debuted and executed it on a Smoky Mountain Wrestling TV taping. I did it on a young Robbie Eagle, who eventually went on to WCW Super-stardom as, "The Maestro." I remember being in the ring with Robbie and blocking his German suplex before slipping under his arm and hooking him with the move. Jim Cornette was doing commentary along with Bob Caudle during that match. Everyone knows what a heel manager Jimmy is and out of

Dean, Larry, & Joe Malenko,
Malenko Wrestling School,
Tampa, Florida.

nowhere he broke character when he "popped" for my finish. "He just did a Northern Light Suplex. Blaze wins the match with a Northern Lights Suplex," or something to that effect. Of course I didn't know this until I watched the playback but I do know it was pretty exciting to do it for the first time in a match. It had worked and I looked damn good doing it. That's not me boasting, that's me being real. No one had done it on TV in the US at that time and it would be a couple of years before others were doing it, at least on a national level.

Anyway, I digress, but that's me, going around the world to cross the sidewalk while telling a story. I had seen Dean work on several local shows throughout Florida when I first started working some shows for the wrestling school and for a couple other guys who ran shows. Once I became a little more advanced, and Larry (Boris Malenko) first began having a couple of health problems, Dean took over my training. I also got to watch Joe Malenko and workout with him some early on as he would come in to work on his timing or ring conditioning before a big Japan tour. I really can't begin to tell you just how talented both were. In the words of Marvin Joel, the man responsible for putting me in touch with The Malenkos way back when he wrote to me saying, "The Malenkos are the best craftsmen in the business." Looking back, truer words were never spoken.

Dean was working on these small shows back then in between tours of Japan, Mexico, Puerto Rico, and 1,000 other places throughout the world. He did shows for the school, helped run shows, and was just about to begin doing more of the training for his father. We had worked on a couple shows together for Sun Coast Pro Wrestling and a few others in Tampa and the surrounding area before he took over my training. Wow, just wow to see him work in the ring. He was ages ahead of everyone else at this time, maybe 1989, and many, on a worldwide level had never heard of him outside of Florida, Japan and a couple other places I mentioned. Of course that would soon change.

I recall the very first time I stepped in the ring with him. He was in the ring with me and a guy I was training with at the time. The guy's name was Larry and he was trying to do a high knee lift and when he did, he kneed me right in the jaw. It felt like he kneed my teeth out, Larry, not Dean. I had my head turned and I couldn't see it coming. Remember; always keep your eyes on your opponent at all times. That's a good way to learn that lesson right there. It only took one time for me to learn it. Always keep your eyes on your opponent.

So, Dean goes on to show Larry how to approach the move, not to rush it, and to relax more while performing it. I'm bent over in the middle of the ring and when Dean, who was now going to execute the move on me, approached, I turned my head. "Bobby, I'm the person you should least be worried about hurting you. I have more experience than anyone here." That was one of the first things he said to me while in the ring. I realized he was right. The other guy was just learning the move but Dean had probably been doing it

97

for ten years at this point. He approached me again from my left, yes I was looking out of the corner of my eyes to see him, and he performed the high knee lift. I didn't feel a thing. He was so light in the ring. Smooth too. He ended up helping each of us that day and many more to come. We ended up riding to some of the shows together around the area and sharing many conversations about the business, working, Japan, and me generally just picking his brain about moves, matches, and many of the other great wrestlers who we got to see as fans growing up.

I couldn't believe, well, yes I could believe all the many talents he had seen through the years growing up in and around the business in Florida during the 60's, 70's, and early 80's, knowing most of the top talent in the world had worked the Florida territory at one time or another.

I can honestly look back with great pride knowing that I had been trained by one of the top professional wrestlers in the world in Dean Malenko. How good was Dean? If you don't know him by now then go look him up on the internet. Go to YouTube and watch Joe and Dean Malenko versus The British Bulldogs from 1989 in Japan. That match was voted tag match of the year that year. While you're there go ahead and watch the Malenko brothers against each other in a singles match. Of course that's not counting the number of outstanding matches he had with Eddie Guerrero, Chris Benoit, Rey Mysterio, and countless others throughout the years. Hell, he was voted by *Pro Wrestling Illustrated* as the number one wrestler in the world in 1997. I doubt you have ever seen a bad Dean Malenko match. I know I haven't and I've probably seen over a thousand of his matches through the years.

As you can tell, I have the utmost respect for Dean. I'm glad to have been one of the guys who Dean helped out and trained through the years. Dean has trained some the best wrestlers in the world. He trained me, Bob Cook, and Sean Waltman, hell, that right there is good company to be in and mention. He helped a young Ken Shamrock, Chad Collyer, and too many others to name unless I just wanted to name drop. I'm sure you'll probably find 1,000 guys who Dean has helped in some way through the years. And, yes, me mentioning the 1,000 this and 1,000 that is an inside rib about him being the man of a thousand holds if you haven't caught on yet.

Dean now works for the WWE and rightfully so. He has a great mind for this business whether it is training, moves, holds, or finishes on matches. He deserves every bit of success he has due to his hard work and persistence in the world of professional wrestling. I'm sure VKM is glad to have Dean on his roster in whatever capacity he may serve: wrestler, trainer, producer, or road agent. Dean is, simply the best!

## ✎ Dan Severn 2.0 ✎

I wrote about the first match I had against Dan "The Beast" Severn in, *Pin Me Pay Me, Have Boots Will Travel*. I probably didn't put the match over as much as I should have as it was actually a pretty good match. Yes, it was a work, but it was about an 80–20 work–shoot. Even though Dan was and is a complete gentleman outside the ring he earned the title of being a, "Beast" inside the ring honestly. He was a Beast! I had respect for him before, during, and after our first match. Severns' credentials speak for themselves. He had been a college All–American, an alternate on the United States Olympic team, and of course, he had won a couple of Ultimate Fighting Championships. In the months that followed our first match and leading up to the second, I gained even more respect for him, as he was training harder to learn the pro style and was also competing and catching on quickly about our business as professionals.

At the time of our first match, I think he had only had three professional wrestling matches after training some with Al Snow. Don't worry Al, I won't hold that against you, but I wish you had smartened him up just a little more. I kid you. Oh, and I'm glad you got a job in SMW after our outstanding match in my hometown of Ashland. We tore the house down that night. Thanks!

The rematch between Dan and me took place in Knoxville, Tennessee at The Civic Coliseum in front of a sold out crowd of about 6,000 fans at SMW's, "Super Bowl of Wrestling" on August 4, 1995. The first match had taken place back in May of that same year in Charlotte, North

Carolina. The card that night was action packed and loaded with big stars from all over the United States. Top talent from SMW, USWA, WCW and the WWF were well represented on this great event. Several guys from the event went on to become WWF/WWE superstars. I was proud to be representing SMW and have another chance to battle for the NWA Heavyweight title. The NWA title had changed through the years, not just in who was champion, but the way it had been presented. But, to me it was always the championship belt of the real world's heavyweight wrestling champion. I take great pride in the fact that I actually had several NWA title shots as this is the belt that is the oldest surviving wrestling championship in the world. I had wrestled Chris Candido for the NWA Heavyweight belt twice, once in my own hometown, and now I had my fourth shot at it as I was going against Severn a second time. Many people don't know these small facts, but to a guy like me, a guy who had been a fan as a kid, and then became a man who pursued his dream of becoming a professional wrestler, well, a World Title shot is just icing on the cake. To me, it was and is, all about pride.

The day before the scheduled match was to take place Severn came through Ashland and paid me a visit. He was on his way to Knoxville, having traveled from Michigan. We ended up going to the local gym and getting a workout in as well as hitting the wrestling mats. He was very professional and understanding as we were just two gentlemen discussing business. As we spoke I explained to him that I had been with Smoky Mountain Wrestling for a few years now and had a good understanding of what the fans there would enjoy in a match and what they expected from a "professional wrestling match." We rolled around a little and fed each other a couple of ideas and pretty much left it at that. What we didn't do was talk about how we would do this spot or that spot. We had a good idea for the opening of the match and the finish and that was it.

On the way to Knoxville the next morning we spoke about many things but we didn't talk much about wrestling. On many of my road trips with the boys through the years it seems we all usually end up talking about what else, but, you guessed it, the business. Well, this wasn't the case with

Severn. I recall he mentioned that he got to wrestle in Russia and other than him saying something about him being able to work a shoot or shoot a work. I always thought that was strange. "I can work a shoot or shoot a work."

Did he think I was going to try to double cross him, or if not me, someone else? Or, was this a challenge to test me or someone else in the future that he may not want to work with? Of course, it could have just been his inner shooter, UFC mentality about the overall business of professional wrestling. I think it was probably the latter as I'm not so sure he ever fully loved and respected professional wrestling the way guys like me did, as I was a fan from early on.

Either way, I was there to work, not shoot. I was there to do business. I also knew that I had a good idea about what the fans in SMW would enjoy. Here would be a good spot for me to tell you the reader just how important a referee is in a professional wrestling match is. Instead of explaining it twice, see the story called questionable tactics. The reason I make mention of it here is because as I said above, we had a good idea what the opening of the match would look like, then go into a match that would involve, kicks, suplexes, and submissions until finally going into a finish.

The very first spot was going to be I would either fireman carry him or he would fireman carry me, and then immediately once the other kicked out, we would do the opposite. He firemen carried me, I kicked out quick, I then in turn firemen carried him and he kicked out quick. It was to be a great, energetic opening spot. The only problem was, the official referee of SMW, Mark Curtis wasn't in the ring with us. It was some fat ass guy, and no I don't recall your name if you ref'd this match and are reading this, but the problem was this fat ass was just getting down for the count when I was to hit mine on Severn, thus the opening was lost in the moment and didn't showcase our wrestling ability and speed to get the spot over. I sincerely think that if Mark had been in there with us, the spot would have gotten over big time. Oh well, anyway, we knew then what we were up against so we just worked until it was time to go home. We didn't have an exact time to go home in or under, but just when we felt it was right. Of course I was pretty much in charge of that as I could gauge the fans. Severn was in charge of that as to how aggressive he was and how we flowed with the action. After the first spot, I threw a few kicks, stiff ones I might add, before he shot in and took me off my feet. We did some chain wrestling in and out of holds and a couple of moves here and there while maintaining a steady pace throughout the match. We worked stiff and hard, but we worked. This match was a lot smoother than the first one as this was more of a complete work. It was also more 50-50 in terms of me being able to do a few more offensive moves on him, unlike before where he was already countering my every move before I even went to make it. This time he let me work into things and then he would counter or try to hit a submission on me. Again, as he did in our first match he went for a Japanese arm bar. This time I slid out of the ring instead of tapping out. This meant something as many knew how the first match had ended, so adding this, only added to the match. It was a good match from a ring psychology point of view. The fans liked it, Dan and I liked it, and I recall walking into the back where several of the boys had been either watching through the curtains or on the monitors and many of them clapped, shook my hand, or just verbally put it over.

I remember seeing Cornette watching a monitor with a couple of others as I turned a corner in the back of the arena. Buddy Landel jumped up out of his seat in front saying, "Bobby that was a hell of a match. You need to send a copy of that to Japan." Buddy and I had worked many, many times together. We had a really good professional and working relationship. I could always tell when Buddy was being Buddy, maybe bullshitting around with someone or when Buddy was being Buddy and being completely serious with someone. I knew the difference. He was sincerely happy that I had had a good match with Severn and he was completely serious about putting me and the match over, and about sending a tape of that match to Japan. I'll never forget that reaction from Buddy.

The match wasn't what I would call a five star match, but it was a damn good match. It was part shoot, part work, but an all-around solid match that served its purpose on this card. After the little mishap on the opening move set, the rest of the match went smoothly as I said. I eventually tried to hit "The Beast" with a stiff clothesline when he caught me in a Fujiwara arm bar. I never minded working snug or stiff in the ring and we did during this match. I laid my kicks in hard as did he. My only concern was when I hit him with that stiff running clothesline was whether or not he was going to rip my arm out of the socket as I was running at him full speed. He hit it just in time as he brought me down to the mat for the submission. The timing was perfect. The fans popped for the finish as expected and as mentioned. Everyone liked the match. That's what this business is all about isn't it, giving the fans their money's worth? They saw a good, hard fought wrestling match between two professional athletes performing at their best. Win, lose, or draw, it just doesn't get any better than that in professional wrestling.

I didn't win, I didn't kick out on two, at least in this match, but I did have one hell of a match for the NWA World Heavyweight Title that night. I had also gone move for move and hold for hold with one legit tough son of a gun that night, and the match got over. Yeah, I can shoot a work or, work a shoot as well my friend. I'm just glad on this night, we worked!

## ❧ Eight ❧

*"Friendship... is not something you learn in school. But if you haven't learned the meaning of friendship, you really haven't learned anything."—Muhammad Ali*

## ❧ Kevin Sullivan ❧

"The Task Master" came to visit me at my home one day. That's right Kevin Sullivan, in the flesh came by for a visit one day a couple years back. He had been booked on some shows nearby. And lucky for me, he was kind enough to pay me a visit even though he had a busy schedule. I had a ring set up and was doing a little seminar while Shane Storm did the actual hands on training. We were helping some younger trainees at the time. It turned out to be a great day as Kevin told several shoot stories about his illustrious career. One of the many things that really stood out while he was talking to Shane Storm and myself, were really about other people and the people he had helped book or build up through the years. Of course this only deepened my respect for Kevin. Think about this. Kevin had the task of going to a 6'6" 320 pound Sid Vicious and asked him to put over a 5'7" 220 Chris Benoit. Kevin had such a tough job as the booker or a booker in WCW, yet he did his job with the utmost respect for the business because he loved the business and believed in it. For those who don't know, Kevin was the one who pulled Bill Goldberg off television for a few months and repackaged him as unbeatable. Goldberg had been beaten before he started his streak. If you recall, he was wearing an Atlanta Falcons jersey and tried to steal Mongo McMichael's Super Bowl Ring or something. But Kevin changed Goldberg's look to a completely shaved head, the plain black wrestling trunks and the short version of black boots like Mike Tyson wore. Think about it as you read this. Kevin Sullivan basically invented Goldberg. Of course, no one knew what was about to happen as Goldberg went over and got so hot that he became a household name at the time, but Kevin helped create the monster. Genius!

The other significant thing that Shane and I both recalled was when I was instructing some students to never take their eyes of their opponent. Think about it, if it's a real fight, you would never take your eyes off the guy you were fighting. Why would you in a wrestling match? Kevin said he didn't know of anyone else that taught that anymore. Well, I am a believer in it. I always try to teach that. Know where your opponent is at all times.

I hadn't seen him in several years and it sure was a pleasure to have him stop by to visit. We talked a little about baseball as it was during the summer, we talked about his Red Sox and my beloved Orioles and how each team was doing. He had a few words of encouragement for me privately, and took the time to speak to a few of the students in the ring working, as well as some lifelong wrestling fans who I had invited over to meet him in person. Not only was I excited by his visit, I was just glad he didn't put me or anyone else in, "The Tree of Woe" that day. Kevin has such a brilliant mind for the wrestling business. Kevin Sullivan was a genius when it came to story lines in pro wrestling. He made it seem real and believable.

*A visit from The Taskmaster.*

I mentioned in my first book about my first in-ring experience with, "The Taskmaster" so I'll keep it brief here. My first time in the ring with Kevin was in SMW in a battle royal. He grabs me, and in a low tone of voice says, "I hear Larry trained you." I quietly spoke back, "Yes sir." "Larry is a good guy and a good trainer. Put your hand on the top of my head." I then placed my hand on the top of his head as he guided himself towards the middle of the ring, and propels himself over the top rope. I couldn't believe it. He was the first man out and I had eliminated him. He was respectful, and professional enough to give this kid a break as he eliminated himself. I felt like I had been treated like a professional and was shown a certain level of respect by a man who I respected, Kevin Sullivan.

I had the utmost respect for him before then and still do to this day. Thanks Kevin for stopping by my house for a visit. It meant more to me than you may ever know. One of the last things he told Shane and me was, "We're not marks Bobby. We are still fans." It was nice spending time with him on a more personal level, but also in a professional manner as well. I only hope our paths cross again soon my friend. Max respect!

## ❧ Terry Taylor ❧

Terry was the person who called me and invited me down to Charlotte for my tryout match with WCW. At first I thought it was a rib, but he assured me that it was him and notified me as to whom to contact for my travel arrangements. He was the one who actually authorized my contract with the company. Terry always made sure that I was placed in good matches and helped me understand what was expected of me while I was there. He always had good opponents lined up for me at the World Wide Tapings that were held in Orlando at Universal Studios. He was always positive and was always giving me positive feedback on my matches. He also paid me one of the best compliments that I received while working in WCW with the other two greatest compliments coming from Arn Anderson. One night Terry came up to me in front of a couple of the other boys and said that I was "one the most underused talents" on the WCW roster. Of course some of, well one of, the higher ups didn't truly appreciate my talents. Many like me had worked for years to craft our ring skills. Terry knew this and understood it. Terry took the time to let me know that he appreciated my talents and that I was one of the guys who wasn't being used to my full potential. It was a nice compliment and I know he was being sincere when he told me this. Thank you Terry for helping me get a job in WCW and also for all the kind compliments and the respect. Much appreciated!

106

## ꙮ Ricky and Robert ꙮ

*"The Rock–n–Roll Express"*

When I think of, "The Rock–n–Roll Express" I think to myself, right there is a show all within itself. Those guys defined what tag–team wrestling is, was, and the way it should be. The next two things that come to mind are Ricky Morton and Robert Gibson, the dynamic duo that make up the R&R Express. I also think back to the great battles they had with Jim Cornette's, "Midnight Express" tag teams. Whew! Man! That's a lot of years ago, but if you're a fan of tag–team wrestling do yourself a favor and go back and watch some of those matches. Still today if I hear, *Old Time Rock & Roll* by Seger on the radio I expect Ricky and Robert to come running out of nowhere, as I can still picture them making their ring entrance.

Lately I've been seeing that the big WWE is now doing more with the tag–team division. I think that's a good thing, and I'm seeing some pretty good performers and matches when I do elect to watch their programming. I hope at some point soon, the, "Rock–n–Roll Express," right there along with the, "Midnight Express" and Cornette to be inducted into the WWE HOF.

Now back to Ricky and Robert. First, both guys are just two of the best guys you could ever meet as a fan, as one of the boys, or just someone who has been to the top. They reached the pinnacle in their chosen profession. Still today they are making towns and are still in touch with their fan base. In other words, these guys are still over today, thirty years after they were put together as a tag–team. Both have been more than generous to me, in and out of the business and in and out of the ring. I've shared hotels with them, traveled with them, been on 1,001 shows with them, worked with and against each of them in singles and in tag matches and I never get over the fact of how down to earth these guys are when it comes to dealing with and knowing their fans.

I remember sitting in a locker room one night and Sandy Scott was talking to me about running a couple of towns for SMW. I had already ran one and had The R&R Express headline it. A few minutes later they both came into the locker room. Sandy says something along the lines of, "These two guys right here. They're the best. No matter if they were on top or working under. No matter if they had money or were selling out buildings and making money, they've never changed. They never let their success go to their head." He knew them a lot longer than I did at this point, but I knew he was speaking the truth in front of the boys. To this day, I'm still friends with both of them and they have never been anything but first class men to me, to the other boys in the locker room, and especially to their fans who still come and see them whenever and wherever they are booked.

I usually get to see them about twice a year and I look forward to it each time I see either one or both of them. Folks, the Rock-n-Roll Express is still out there on the road, and I'm sure Ricky Morton will tell you on any given night, "The fans were hanging from the rafters" to watch their match. Get out there and hang from the rafters too and see these two still

*Tracy Smothers, Bobby Blaze, & The Rock-N-Roll Express.*

in action after all these years. On a side note, if you're one of the boys and have the privilege to work with them or get to hear a story or two from them, consider yourself one lucky person.

They still give back to the business through their respected wresting schools and by giving sound advice to up and coming wrestlers on a regular basis. I could write an entire chapter on each or as a team, but I just don't have room in this book for that, but I want each of them to know this: Ricky, Robert, if you're reading this or word gets back to you about my mention of you, just know, I have nothing but max respect and love for each of you. Thanks for all that you have done for me through the years, but more importantly, thanks for the many years of friendship.

## Tim Horner

It was shortly after I had my tryout match with SMW that I finally got to meet Tim Horner or "White Lightning" Tim Horner as he was known during those days. I think Tim is a wonderful guy. He was always as respectful to me as I was him. I had seen Tim working on TV and house shows for both WCW and the WWF for years. I always thought he was a very talented worker. One night, and this was shortly after meeting him in person while backstage at a SMW show, I brought up a match I watched him have with Barry Horowitz. He remembered the match I was talking about. This would have been prior to the days of WWE/RAW shows, but it was a WWF show none the less. They really let both guys work that night and both of them were good workers. I don't care how many jobs they may have done in the past, on this night they got to actually work. By the way, just in case you didn't already know, I hate the word, "jobber," but, just like in real life we all have jobs to do. Always remember, no matter what your job is, always try to give it your best effort. That applies to anything in any field, career, or job.

It's no big secret that Barry has done thousands of jobs throughout his career, but, Barry could work. Tim and Barry put on a wrestling clinic that night and as I said, Tim remembered it and thanked me for the compliment. Of course I had seen him working with Brad Armstrong on TBS when they were both with the NWA/WCW back in the day as well and knew he could work. I enjoy professional wrestling, and matches like the ones I mentioned, well, they excite me. I like it when two talented guys get to actually work a match and tell a story in the ring. I'm adding Tim Horner's name to this book, because I probably didn't give him enough credit in my last book and feel like he deserves a lot of credit for helping me while in SMW. A few things come to mind when I think of Tim other than what I've already mentioned. One was, when they put the SMW World JR Heavyweight Title on me to start my program with Candido, I went up to thank

Tim for the opportunity and he shook my hand, looked me in the eye, and said, "I told you, we all like you here Bobby. You're a good fit."

That made me feel really good about myself and made me want to work that much harder to prove that I did deserve to be there and to represent not only that title, but the company as well. The other couple of things were, I eventually got to do a three or four day loop with Tim up in West Virginia and Virginia where we had a baby face versus baby face match each night. It was like a night off in the ring to work with him, and all of those matches went so smoothly. It was really an honor to work with him and learn from him each night. We actually got to work, and each night we did something a little different, from the basic mat wrestling to a couple of high spots, to just working for a good solid finish each night. Many times, more often than not, having a baby face versus baby face match can be hard to pull off. Fans, especially back then usually liked the typical villain versus the good guy, or classic heel versus baby face matches. However, I think the people who paid their hard earned cash on those nights got their money's worth watching our matches as well as the rest of the matches on the card. I don't think we called one spot, and the only thing I knew going into the ring was his roll up with a bridge going into the pin would be the finish. "We're all just telling a story in the ring Bobby. We all tell it a little differently at times, but we're just telling a story." That's what he told me nightly in the locker room after thanking me for putting him over cleanly in the middle of the ring each night. Tim, it was my pleasure.

## ⚓ Tracy Smothers ⚓

Tracy Smothers was another one of the guys who really helped me out a lot when I came into SMW. He was one of the baby faces for the company. Tracy, along with Ricky and Robert, was one of the guys who smartened me up quick about, "The gimmick table wars." When I first started with SMW, I was lucky enough to just have a handful of pictures with me at the time, but it was from that handful of pictures that I caught on quick. Anything Goes! It was like a flea market out there. I sold fifteen pictures that I had in Johnson City, Tennessee, and immediately upon returning home I went and had a bunch of photos developed and set up another photo shoot for newer and updated pictures. I'm glad I did. There are probably not enough good things I could say about how much Tracy helped me out during our time together in SMW. I'm also glad to say that whenever, "The Wild Eyed Southern Boy" is in my area, it's always a pleasure to see him and hang out with him if only for a few hours. Just like The R&R Express, Tracy can still be seen out there on the local indie shows today. If you see him, ask about wrestling a bear or any other number of things he did during his career. He's one of the good ol' boys in the business and you just don't find them like that anymore.

## ❧ Rick Newsome ❧

There's a guy who's a good friend of mine who I mentioned in my last book, his name is Rick Newsome. The good thing about Rick is he understands the nature of the wrestling business. I first met him at some local matches. I then started training and working out with him some. Well, now it's my turn to, "Put him over one more time," as I put myself over on him in the first book. Ha! Thanks Rick! Yeah, he helped me a lot before I ever went down to train with The Malenkos. Rick took me under his wing by helping with my early training, taking me to shows, and getting me booked on several shows early on. As you may or may not know, I had my very first professional wrestling match in Haysi, Virginia on September 11, 1988. That match was against Rick Newsome from Virgie, Kentucky. I'll never forget that experience. After messing around and trying to learn to work for several

*Rick Newsome with me on September 11, 2013. Twenty—five years to the day, after our first match together.*

111

months and several matches later I spoke with Rick about me going to get some more training as I explained to him I wanted to do the business full time.

I just didn't feel like there were a great many opportunities where I was living at the time and thought it would be best to move on down to Florida. Rick encouraged me in my move and wished me nothing but the best of luck and much success. Of course, that wasn't the last that I saw of him. Through the years we continued to get booked on some of the same shows and ended up working lots of indie shows together. Something else that I'll never forget was when he showed up at my house twenty-five years later, on September, 11, 2013 to personally pick up his copy of, *Pin Me Pay Me*. We spent several hours together just getting caught up on everything that was going on in our lives at the time. Rick was always in the field of law enforcement and has had a long and successful career in his chosen field. I have the utmost respect for him. He is a good man, as honest as the day is long, and I probably can't say enough good things about him. Rick, just know I appreciate you. Thanks for taking a chance on helping me break into the business when it was hard to break into. I am forever grateful my friend.

That was just a small list of some of the guys I have gotten to know through the years. I could go on and on and maybe even drop in more and more, "Big Names" but I can't mention everyone in one book or two. There's a bunch of the boys and many people who I made mention of in the stories throughout the book. If we have ever shared a locker room or shared the ring together, thank you as well. There are a lot of guys who made it to the top or have been to the top of professional wrestling that I was honored to share the ring with. There were others who maybe only had a few matches, and maybe you fit in somewhere in between: If you're one of the boys, thank you. Take care of each other out there on the road and in the ring. You'll look back one day and be glad you did. I know I am, as I had the opportunity to live my dream. Good luck in living yours.

## ⊰ Nine ⊱

*"Whenever I think of the past, it brings back so many memories."—Steven Wright*

## ⊰ Jake's Snake on the Loose ⊱

While on the Wrestle Riot tour, back in 1993 Jake "The Snake" Roberts was getting over big time. He was one of the main big stars on the tour. The promoters had hired someone who had several snakes that they agreed to rent out as the snake that Jake had been using had died somewhere along the trip. Jake had been down in Puerto Rico prior to his arrival in Australia. I'm not sure if the snake died in transit or if it died once we had started the tour. All I know is they had to find a replacement snake for the tour. I think they rented a couple of snakes from a lady who was tied in with a circus or some other type of entertainment performance where snakes where used doing the act. Anyway, they did find a snake for the tour for Jake to carry to the ring.

The tour was taking place in February of that year and it was summer time in Australia, so it was hot. Whether you have ever been into a locker room area or not, it's important to know that many locker rooms can get very hot, especially when you have several grown men all gathered into a small area. Well, apparently for a reptile like a snake it can be even hotter if you're shoved or stuffed it into a dark canvas bag and have been shuffled around from town to town day in and day out.

During the tour prior to several of the shows they had a little meet and greet for the fans. Other times, as it is with most shows, the wrestlers all arrive at least an hour prior to the show. Since we were traveling together by air from show to show, and then taking a tour bus once we reached the town we were to work in several hours prior to the start of each show, we all arrived several hours ahead of show time. We had about twenty wrestlers, a couple of tour managers and promoters, and a couple others in our travel circle for the duration of the tour. Since we all arrived early there were card games, guys just hanging out around the locker room or taking a look around the arenas, or as I said at a meet and greet. Anyway, while no one was in the locker room the snake somehow escaped his canvas bag and was on the loose somewhere in the building. Seeing as how a python crawling around is hard to miss, you would think it might be easy to locate. Well, after Jake discovered that the python wasn't in the bag, everyone in the locker room area began looking around the immediate area, and then around the back stage area without finding even a trace of the snake. No one had a clue where this 15 foot serpent had slithered or disappeared to. As the saying goes in show business, "The show must go on," and go on it did. There were several matches before Jake was scheduled to work his match and the show started and everything went fine. The only problem was the promoters were trying to come up with some kind of a gimmick to stuff into the bag that would resemble the body or shape of a snake. They came up with some type of tubing; it was like a thick vacuum hose. I know it was a tube–shaped structure like they use for underground drainage that was thick enough and then cut into about a 12–15 foot section that could be coiled up and placed in the bag. Of course Jake, being one of the great minds of the wrestling business, could use the bag and still work it as if the actual snake was inside of it. He would carry it to the ring, place it at ringside after teasing or tormenting his opponent prior to and during the match. A finish was worked out so he didn't have to actually produce the snake, in fact, I think someone going down to ringside and running off with the bag is what they ended up doing during the finish.

While the show was taking place, as I mentioned, several wrestlers had already had their match and were hanging out in the locker room. Myself, I always found a place to stand or sit out of view of the fans and just watched the matches and tried to learn something new each and every night of the tour. This would pay off for me in the future, especially when I first started working for Smoky Mountain Wrestling when on one of my first nights there I was watching through the curtain.

While watching, Sandy Scott stopped by me and asked, "What are you doing kid?" I told him I was watching the matches and trying to learn what some of the other guys were doing in their matches. I said, "I'm trying to see what's getting over and what's not getting over in the ring." He looked at me, patted my back and said, "Good kid, you're doing your homework," as he gave me a slight smile before walking on. It's really important for guys to watch the matches on the shows they're on. You can watch from the back, from up in a secluded area of the building or arena, or even on a monitor if there's one available. Just don't be a goof and go sit in the front row like an idiot if you already worked an earlier match. Even in WCW, some of the best workers there would watch the monitors and see what other guys were doing in their matches. You can never learn too much, and you can see what others are doing so you don't go out and do the same thing as another guy earlier in the show or also, as I said, see what's getting over and what's not.

So, anyway, I'm standing there in the back, behind the curtain, as are several other guys who have already worked their match just taking in the show when out of nowhere, "OH SHIT!!!" Yes, a loud yell was heard coming from the shower area as a buck naked Keiichi Yamada, better known as Jushin "Thunder" Liger comes running out holding a towel yelling, "Snake! Snake!" The python had apparently gone down into one of the pipes or down through the toilet and had reemerged up through the shower drain while Liger was in the locker room shower area. It was quite a sight to see grown men scrambling around trying to get away and to stay away from that side of the room, as the lady that had rented the snake went into the shower and gently picked it up and loved on it prior to placing it back inside the canvas bag. This just happened while Jake was out working his match so it was already too late to get the actual snake worked into the match, but the match went as planned and the finish came off perfectly, again, just as planned. Once the promoter and the snake lady, who had been very nervous and rightfully upset, as this was her pet, talked things out, she continued to rent the snake out for the remainder of the tour and the snake only came out of the bag when it was necessary. So, that's the story of how one night in Australia Jake's snake got loose, or at least the only time his "gimmick" snake got loose, whether his other snake ever got loose or not, well, that's a completely different story.

"As good as I was at wrestling; I never thought I was good enough." Jake Roberts. You're right Jake. You weren't good. You were GREAT! I'm glad to hear you're doing so much better these days. One day at a time.

## ◅৯ Lady T ৯◅

Through the years I've helped train many young talents breaking into the pro wrestling business. There's a long list of people who I have helped in some small way through the years. I always took pride in the fact that I had been trained by The Malenkos and even had the opportunity to be a trainer there myself back in the day. So, I always trained others with what I and many others call, "The Malenko Way." I don't know that anyone nowadays does the conditioning aspect of the training like I did when I broke in, but I always start with lockups, wing locks, and basic wrestling moves before eventually letting someone hit the ropes or take a bump. I've seen many guys begin, what they think is professional training and on day two they're taking a suplex or some other crazy shit. That is not proper professional training.

While working out at Malenko's, I helped two young Australian boys, Greg Smit and Mark Mercedes. The first day upon their arrival, my old training partner and tag-team partner, Rico Frederico, and I picked them up at Tampa International Airport. People these days won't travel an hour down the road to train or take a seminar, yet, I've seen guys travel thousands of miles to train in Tampa, myself included. I've seen guys arrive weekly from Japan just to be trained by Malenko. Dean had been doing most of the training by the time I'm writing about and I owe so much to him for his training and also for advice he gave me once we were on the road together in WCW. I was always asking him for advice and he always had sound advice. Anyway, Mark and Greg, even after this long, probably thirty plus hours of flights, stops, layovers, and more flights, were tired and ready for some shut eye, but they both insisted on going by the camp and seeing the gym and the rings that they had so longed to

116

be in. They arrived on a Sunday, and weren't scheduled to start training until Tuesday, but they had to go see the wrestling rings right then. Greg did some work in Japan for Pancreas after some further training from Karl Gotch on down the road. Mark helped start the International Wrestling Australia promotion and still owns it today. He has toured all over the world including, Germany, Japan, and throughout the United States.

I lost touch with Greg years ago, but Mark and I still keep in touch. It was through Mark that I eventually had a young boy; years later named Rob Matrix come stay in my home, train with me, and learn his craft. I'm very proud of the wrestling careers that Mark and Robert ended up having. I'm also proud to say that they are still my friends and have visited me a couple of times and stayed in my home with my family.

I also helped several guys from West "By God" Virginia break into the business. I don't want to leave anyone off or out, but I helped, "Buzz Saw" Brian Jones get his start back in the day. He worked several really good shows with me through the years and we shared many good times on the road together.

Another really good guy who I had the pleasure of training was Bill Bitner, professionally known as "Death Falcon Zero." William Bitner even wrote a graphic novel about DFZ. If you ever get the chance to check out *Death Falcon Zero Vs The Zombie Slug Lords* do so. And yes, Bobby Blaze is immortalized in a graphic novel, so I got that going for me. Thanks Bill. He has also published several other books through the years. He was a good wrestler and worker but an even better man. I'm really glad that I met him and had a part in getting him started in pro wrestling.

Before getting onto the story about Lady T, I want to mention two other young talents I had a hand in helping early on in their careers. Both of them were from West Virginia as well. I first met Kris Brown and Matt Wolfe at a local show, if I recall correctly, it was at a fund raiser event that I was working on during my indie days. My version is a little different from the way Matt recalls it, so you believe whoever you want. I remember being out at the gimmick tables and when they walked by I asked these two young fans if they would be interested in training in the future to become professional wrestlers. I could tell they were loyal fans, but they also seemed to be smartened up some by the way they were getting into the matches. So, being the gentleman I am, I probably said, "Hey guys, would you be interested in getting some professional training in the future?" I'm pretty sure that's what I said. If you ask Matt, and his memory is more than likely much better than mine, so again, believe who you will, Matt claims the question was more direct and more like, "So, do you think you can fuckin' do it?" Anyway, a conversation was struck up and after agreeing to meet several weeks later, Kris and Matt began their training. Kris had a lot of talent and worked all around the area as a baby face known as Kris King. Matt became Shane Storm. He has wrestled all over the US and even did a tour with DFZ down in Mexico. He still stays booked and is very active today working every weekend in a town near you. I'm proud to call him a friend and we have traveled some and taken in many shows together through the years. In addition to the local indie shows we went backstage to a live TNA event and hung out before taking in the matches. We also got first class treatment by getting backstage passes at a WWE house show courtesy of Charles Robinson and Scott Armstrong. Folks, think what you will about the WWE, but they are a first class company. We enjoyed the interaction in the back as well as some pretty outstanding matches that night. The WWE is loaded with top talented guys and girls who are real athletes and enjoy entertaining their fans.

Now back to the story of Lady T. Way back when I was wrestling for SMW we had several monthly towns. I always enjoyed the monthly towns because the fans were so good to the boys. I met so many fans, some who have even become friends through the years. It's always nice to still hear from those fans today. One young fan I met was a deaf girl named Teena from Paintsville, Kentucky. Teena was at about all the shows when we came through that area of Kentucky. I didn't know her name but through her friend and through sign language she always spoke to me and was just real nice. Several years later she inquired about training to become a female wrestler. I was skeptical at first and wasn't sure if she was serious. I wasn't sure if I could give her the kind of help and training she was seeking. We stayed in touch for several months until she bugged me enough that I finally thought, "Why not?"

I also thought if she was serious, she would need to be conditioned. I did this because I wanted to train her in a way that others wouldn't try to take advantage of her in the ring. The first several sessions of training consisted of nothing but conditioning. I had her doing pushups, squats, and neck bridges and never once did she complain.

Once we started to actually wrestle I made her ear bleed unaware that she had her hearing aids in. She didn't say a word. She simply stopped, took them out and told me to treat her like I would anyone else that I trained. For the record, I didn't try to hurt her when I was teaching her a simple head lock, and I wasn't trying to be stiff, it was just that the hearing aids were there, and it was a good lesson for both of us to learn.

She would have to wrestle without them, so I would train her without having to talk too much, but more by showing her the techniques over and over again and it's during this early time in training when one gets those reps in over and over again, so it paid off for her. Again, never once during her training did Teena complain.

Eventually, I let her come into the back, in a separate area to let her manage one of the guys on the local shows. We came up with the gimmick name, "Lady T." She always dressed real nice and did a good job as a valet, but this girl had trained to actually do matches, and it was only a matter of time before she would have one.

By this time SMW had shut down and I was running monthly shows in a couple of the towns, mainly Ashland and Paintsville, Kentucky and a couple of towns in West Virginia and Southern Ohio. I wasn't getting rich, but I was still making good money working the indies and running my own shows. I was also making trips to Japan during this time. I was hoping, but wasn't sure at this time that I would get into WCW, which, as you all know, I eventually did. The business was changing that's for sure.

Anyway, at the time I was working a lot for Les Thatcher and Heartland Championship Wrestling out of Cincinnati, Ohio. Les had several young guys who were working regularly for me and after several months of in house angles in Ashland, it was time for Lady T to have a match. We did a deal where each month a manager would make fun of Lady T as a valet which of course was going to lead up to her challenge. The manager was a smaller guy but he also knew how to work. Lady T was a valet and they had heat during a few matches in which they would get involved and that would eventually lead up to a match in the future. It would be an "intergender match." Wonder where the booker got that idea?

On the night that Lady T was to make her debut we still didn't have another girl and didn't advertise an intergender match but we kept going straight ahead with the idea of her and the manager working each other in a match. I think he used the name, "GQ" or something like that and as I said he was actually a pretty good worker. But then again, who couldn't work if Les Thatcher had anything to do with their training? Les is still one of the top trainers in the business today doing seminars and such. He knows our business inside and out. Besides that, he's a really great guy. The referee for the match was a guy named Dean Roll; he was also a darn good worker who you may know better as, "Shark Boy."

I was down at the announcers table doing an interview when I called out Lady T. She of course had to be told to come down to the table by several of the other wrestlers. I spoke to her and told her that she couldn't have her planned match that night as no girls were available to wrestle her. Remember folks, "card subject to change," but I assured her that she could manage and we would try to get her a match the following month. Well, about this time, the manager, we'll just call him, "G" comes walking down the length of the gym floor using a walker none the less and wearing a neck brace, a knee brace, and an elbow pad. It seemed as if it took him twenty minutes to get to the announcers table where he asked if he could please speak to Lady T. After I handed him the microphone, he said, "Lady T, look at me. I'm handicapped. I'm handicapped just like you. I don't know if you can hear me or not. But, I hope you can hear me, so listen, I have bad knees and need this walker. I have an injured neck, and need this neck brace. I'm sorry I made fun of you all this time, but now I understand what it's like to be handicapped. I'm a handicapped person just like you!"

When he said that, Lady T jerked the microphone from his hand, and he just about stumbled over the walker when she did. She said, "I might not hear everything you say but, I'm not handicapped! Now here's something I do know you can hear! So HEAR THIS!" She slammed the mic down and flipped him off with her middle finger and turned to walk toward the ring.

Everyone was laughing, clapping, a hootin' and a hollerin' and after she got about ten steps away from him and about half way to the ring, G picked up that walker, and started running after her and smashed it right across her back. It was awesome as the walker busted into four or five pieces and she hit the gym floor like a ton of bricks had fallen on her back and head. She took one hell of a bump; of course she really had no choice because she got blasted with that walker. G then picked her up and helped get her into the ring and proceeded to beat the snot out of her. He was beating her from pillar to post and back. The crowd was going nuts. They were booing, they were yelling for the ref to stop it. They were yelling for guys in the back to come out to help, it was pure chaos as he beat her down. It was getting the reaction and the heat we wanted it to get. This went on for about four or five minutes, just enough to get it over to the max. Then G shot Lady T into a turnbuckle and charged her at full force. At the last second and out of desperation she moved. He sold it and turned and sat right back into the turnbuckle. Lady T now with the fans chanting her name and cheering her on gathered her wits and saw her one and only opportunity. She turned, lined him up and, BAM, she kicked him right between the legs. Now I hate nut shots during matches, but this one had meaning. It actually made sense for her to deliver a swift kick in the nuts. G had no choice but to sell it and fell right out into the middle of the ring. By this time the people were with it and standing on their feet with many even up closer than normal to ring side.

121

Lady T fell down on top of G for the pin and for an added effect the lady running the concession stand even jumped up and laid on across G as well for the one, two, three count and the win. Chalk one up for the good guys, or in this case the little deaf girl no one believed in but me.

During this time, and the entire time of her training she never complained once about her hearing, the physical training, and the hours she spent traveling to and from Ashland to train. I think that says a lot for Teena "Lady T" Fannin. I'm proud to still call her my friend to this day. So, Teena, if you can hear me, or are at least reading this, professional wrestling needs more people like you, dedicated and hard-working people who are willing not only to pay their dues but also to do whatever it takes to make it in pro wrestling.

### ✎ Cotton Candy ✎

I used to always like cotton candy, the one memory of it that comes to mind is when I was young and you used to be able to buy it cheap at K-Mart. It was a real treat if my mom would buy me some when I was a young kid. But there was one kind of cotton candy I didn't like, and that was a guy named Cotton Candy. I can't remember his real name or his working name, but he was this young guy who was friends with a promoter I worked for pretty regularly somewhere down in Kentucky near the Cumberland Gap area. There used to be a monthly show there and it drew really well and actually had some good talent and matches on the shows. The guy promoting whose name also slips my mind would use a couple of guys from SMW and me on a regular basis. I wish I could remember his name, but if I did, that would require me to remember his partner's name as well, then I would have to remember his partner's wife's name who the first guy or partner was sleeping with at the time, and then of course, when the guy came to me upset telling me that his girlfriend was still sleeping with her husband and he was upset about it, and it might make him quit being partners with his friend and that would result in having to shut down his little monthly wrestling show. I'm not sure whatever happened to any of them, but I think the promoter's story

122

went something like this: "My buddy told me he had some bad news for me. I asked what he meant, and he said, 'your wife is cheating on both of us.'" I knew then that my bookings weren't going to last much longer with this little outlaw group. Anyway, they had this guy who was a manager, and he did a pretty good job. He would get some heat during the introduction and then come out and work with whoever was in their main event that night. The guys who had been on television, from either the USWA or SMW, apparently weren't good enough to work the main events, but hey, our names helped build their crowd, and again, the payoffs were pretty good, so it didn't matter to me if I worked in the opening match or the semi-main event, I usually kicked out on two, got the win, got my pay and hit the next town. It was business—only for me.

So anyway, this manager had this big ol' fuzzy head of blond hair and the fans all ended up nick naming him Cotton Candy. He was built like a lollipop stick, but instead of a sucker on top, okay, maybe he was a sucker, I don't know, but he had a head of cotton candy looking hair on top of his lollipop body. You get the picture. Anyway, one night I was standing behind my gimmick table trying to sell pictures, tee-shirts, etc. to make a little extra travel and food money when this old man of about 70 comes right through the line and shouts, "I ought to shoot you!" He was a big old guy too. I can still see him now in is Sunday best, bibbed blue jean overalls with a white tee-shirt complete with fresh tobacco spit stains. Being a "baby face" laughing, joking, selling and taking pictures with the small crowd at my table I didn't really think he was talking to me, until, as I said, he burst through a couple of girls, well young ladies, who were talking to me, and he repeated, "I ought to shoot you. By God, I'll go to my truck and get my gun right now you son of a bitch." As he gets to within striking distance he already has his knife out and still cussing. By now, I realize he's talking to me, but I've stepped back enough that he can't reach across the table to cut me. I was more concerned about him cutting one of the girls I had been talking to than myself, so unless he threw the knife or actually already had a gun on him, I was pretty much out of harm's way. Again, thinking about the people and the girls being that close, I was more worried about them until I heard one of them say, "Daddy, that's not him!" "I'll kill you!" By now, both girls, and when I say girls, these were ladies, both probably in their late twenties to early thirties, so I'm not talking about little girls here, but they both start, saying over and over to him, and he was red in the face, cussin' and spitting baccer juice all over the place as they pleaded, "Daddy it's not him."

Now I knew this man wasn't mad about me talking to his daughters, there was nothing going on there, but I still didn't know what this old farmer's problem was with me to make him want to cut me or go get his gun and shoot me. Hell, he may have thought I had been messing around with one of sheep or something, I had no clue. Anyway, the two girls get him calmed down, the one and only policeman who was standing not too far away had come over by this time as well, asking people what's going on, and talking to the girls and the old timer. Once the dust settled down and as more and more people tried to find out what had caused the outburst, many started laughing, talking, and saying it's alright to each other, to the policeman, the old man and me. By now, he was calm as a kitten, as he reached out his hand to shake mine and to apologize to me. I still didn't really know what was said or what had happened before this gesture. One of the girls started speaking to me as I extended my hand to the old man. "He thought you were Cotton Candy. He hates that little bastard." "I'm sorry sir, I'm sorry bout that," he said as he shook my hand. "I didn't know." By now, it was closer to show time or at least time to make my way to the back. I'm not sure if I would have sold many pictures to some of the people or fans in my line, but I think I was more than compensated for the twenty minutes or so of chaos. After apologizing, he bought each of the daughters a couple of my pictures, each of them a tee-shirt, and even a Bobby Blaze hat for himself. I might have not liked the name Cotton Candy that night, but I think Bobby Blaze gained at least one more fan, plus an extra fifty or so dollars in gimmick sales from an old farmer in Kentucky, and in my book that beats getting stabbed or shot anytime.

Cotton candy, or whatever your real or gimmick name is, thank you for getting so much heat that you got me threatened, but also for the gimmick sales that night. I sure as hell hope you have done something with that head of hair of yours. We never, and I mean never looked anything alike except our hair was blonde. Mine was at least clean and well groomed, and yours, well it looked like dirty cotton candy that had been dropped and then picked back up at the county fair. I hate cotton candy!

LESSON PLAN - FULL TIME

Larry Malenko's PRO WRESTLING
SCHOOL ITINERARY

#1   STRETCHING DRILLS
     COLLAR & ELBOW - LOCK UP
     FORWARD ROLL BUMP DRILL
     HEAD LOCK
     STANDING WRISTLOCK
     STANDING WRISTLOCK TAKEDOWN
     HEADLOCK TAKEDOWN
     WINGLOCK TAKEDOWN

#2   STRETCHING DRILLS
     FORWARD ROLL BUMP DRILL
     REVIEW LESSON #1
     MEXICAN ARM DRAG TAKEDOWN
     FRONT FACELOCK TAKEDOWN
     GO BEHIND FROM LOCK UP - STANDING SWITCH
     GO BEHIND TAKEDOWN FROM LOCK UP

#3   STRETCHING DRILLS
     BUMP DRILLS & BEGIN BACK BUMPS
     REVIEW LESSONS #1 & #2
     HAMMERLOCK FROM LOCK UP - REVERSE HAMMERLOCK
     DROP TOE HOLD
     HEADLOCK SWITCH/HAMMERLOCK/LEG TAKEDOWN

#4   STRETCHING DRILLS
     REVIEW LESSONS #1,#2,#3
     REGULAR ARM DRAG FROM LOCK UP & BRIDGE
     MEXICAN ARM DRAG FROM LOCK UP & BRIDGE

#5   STRETCHING DRILLS
     INTRODUCTION TO HITTING RING ROPES
     REVIEW LESSONS #1,#2,#3,#4
     REVERSE TOP WRISTLOCK TO HAMMERLOCK
     ARM WHIP & REVERSE ARM WHIP
     ARM BAR

#6   STRETCHING DRILLS
     HITTING RING ROPES DRILL
     REVIEW LESSONS #1,#2,#3,#4,#5
     FIREMAN'S CARRY TAKEDOWN
     SNAPMARE TAKEDOWN
     SNAPMARE TAKEDOWN TO REAR CHINLOCK
     HIPLOCK TAKEDOWN

#7   STRETCHING DRILLS
     RUNNING ROPES DRILL(JUMPING OVER OPPONENT)
     REVIEW LESSONS #1,#2,#3,#4,#5,#6
     LEG SWEEP TAKEDOWN
     SINGLE LEG SWEEP TAKEDOWN
     DOUBLE LEG SWEEP TAKEDOWN

----------------------------------------------------------------
#8    STRETCHING DRILLS
      RUNNING ROPES DRILL(JUMPING OVER 1 THEN 2 OPPONENTS)
      REVIEW LESSONS #1,#2,#3,#4,#5,#6,#7
      STEP OVER TOE HOLD
      SINGLE LEG BOSTON CRAB
----------------------------------------------------------------
#9    STRETCHING DRILLS
      RUNNING ROPES DRILL(JUMPING OVER 1 THEN 2 OPPONENTS)
      REVIEW LESSONS #1,#2,#3,#4,#5,#6,#7,#8
      LEAP FROG OPPONENT OFF ROPES
      SIT OUT
      SIT OUT/SIT OUT SWITCH
      SIT OUT/TURN IN
----------------------------------------------------------------
#10   STRETCHING DRILLS
      INTRODUCE LEAP FROG & PANCAKE DRILLS
      REVIEW LESSONS #1,#2,#3,#4,#5,#6,#7,#8,#9
      BODY SLAM
      BACK BREAKER
      SIDE BACK BREAKER
      SMALL PACKAGE/COUNTER FROM BODY SLAM
      SHOULDER BREAKER
----------------------------------------------------------------
#11   STRETCHING DRILLS
      LEAP FROG & PANCAKE DRILL
      REVIEW LESSONS #1 - #10
      PROPER WAY TO COVER OPPONENT & KICK OUT FROM PIN
      DOUBLE WRISTLOCK TAKEDOWN
      BEEL THROW FROM TURNBUCKLES
----------------------------------------------------------------
#12   STRETCHING DRILLS
      LEAP FROG & PANCAKE DRILL
      REVIEW LESSONS #1 - #11
      BACK DROP
      SUNSET FLIP PINNING MOVE
      KNEE LIFT
----------------------------------------------------------------
#13   STRETCHING DRILLS
      LEAP FROG & PANCAKE DRILL
      REVIEW LESSONS #1 - #12
      DOUBLE UNDER HOOK SUPLEX
      GUT WRENCH SUPLEX
      SIDE SUPLEX
      VERTICLE SUPLEX
----------------------------------------------------------------
#14   STRETCHING DRILLS
      REVIEW LESSONS #1 - #13
      WHIPPING & REVERSING OPPONENT INTO TURNBUCKLES
      MONKEY FLIP FROM TURNBUCKLES
      TAKING & DELIVERING SHOULDER TACKLES
      HIP TOSS & REVERSE HIP TOSS OFF ROPES

127

# ❧ Ten ❧

*"Give me chastity and continence, but not yet."*
St. Augustine

## ❧ Eros Theater & Bookstore ❧

Eros Theater: So I'm in this adult movie theater/bookstore, you know the kind, where they have those small booths that you can deposit a couple of bucks in and there's always that strong smell of, well, Okay, you get my drift. I go into a booth and surf through a few channels just to get my coins' worth of viewing pleasure but I didn't actually find a suitable movie. I did however see some interesting foreign films that catered to certain fetishes. Quite interesting, just not my cup of pee, oops, tea. I come out and continue to stroll around the shop and that's when I spot a special row of booths where, once inside, you can actually watch a live performer. Now we're talking. This is right up my alley, or is it down my alley? Either way, I was in the right alley. Again, you know the kind, dark, kind of narrow and with a certain amount of mystery to it before you decide to take a walk down it. So I go in, lock my door, insert a few more dollars, and wallah, a window opens and there's a panel of glass with a speaker hole and on the other side of that glass is a beautiful girl dancing for a select audience, i.e.: other idiots who pay good hard earned money to see a girl dance nude. I can look through the glass and see other male faces also looking on as the dancer walks up to window after window performing for a brief time while trying to sucker them out of a tip. I'll have none of that. I already paid to get my window opened. After she dances her way towards my window, I'm already reaching into my fanny pack. Hey, it was the 90's everyone had a fanny pack, fag bag, or whatever it's called strapped to their waist like the world heavyweight champion title belt. Something besides elastic had to hold up our Zubaz pants. Anyway, I'm fishing out money because I already know I'm donating to this girl's college fund. Forget the previous "sucker" line. As she approaches and speaks to me, I'm not even sure I got a hello out. I think I went right to one of my favorite and easiest pickup lines, "How Much?" She says, "Ten dollars for

128

a dance right here for you, thirty five for a more private one in the back." I quickly slip two fives into the slot, not the slit, but the slot and say, "Lemme see what ya got."

I'm quite sure other services were provided if the right price was negotiated, but I was content for my private dance for now. And we're off. This girl starts dancing right in front of my window. Oh how I pity those fools not getting to see this up close and personal through the other windows. First her bra comes off to the most impressive pair of firm tits money can buy. Those puppies were nice. But I'm a leg man, so I have to see more. A slow hypnotic dance continues until her black lace panties come down and off. "Now we're talking baby," I mumble through my speaker. I'm already trying to pull out my, wait, I'm already trying to locate more ones and fives from my fanny pack. So anyway, her panties are gone, and she is close enough to touch, and maybe even smell, not sure I wanted to, if it wasn't for the glass. "Lemme see that ass," I say a little louder into the speaker. She flashes up a five finger salute and I kindly throw five ones into the gimmick holder and she scoops them up, tosses them on the floor and continues to dance; only now she has her ass right up against the glass while saying little naughty things to me in a very seductive way. I think this girl just might like me. And, yes, my excitement is beginning to mount on my side of the glass. The fanny pack has been pushed out a few more inches from my body if you know what I mean. Oh, to be that young again, and innocent too, "um cough cough" ha–ha.

But, being a leg man as I mentioned I have to see more. After all she still has those sexy black high heels on, and I love perfect legs. Perfect legs you might ask? Perfect legs are the kind of legs that have feet on one end and pussy on the other. I've already seen the other, it was shaved. Being a connoisseur of fine female feet, can you dig that Quentin Tarantino, I have to see this girl's feet. "Take off your shoes."

From the other side of the glass comes a confused look as the dancer moves closer to the speaker, pulls her dark hair back a little and says, "What?" "Take off your shoes; I wanna see your feet baby." A slight nod takes place and she continues to dance a little further from my now slowly closing window. "Fuck," thinking out loud and reaching for yet more five spots to slip into the gimmick box. As I do, the window once again opens, and there she is, my sexy little dark eyed beauty dancing away for my delight. But, she still has those high heels on. "Take off your shoes!" I say it a little louder this time until she moves back up against the glass, and this time, in an even louder voice, "Take off those shoes!" Ah, the excitement was a building, so close... She then removes her shoes to reveal a sexy pair of feet. She had a nice pedicure. Her toes were polished off in a wonderful bright whore-red color that just drives me crazy. Houston, we have lifted off...and blast off!!! I stick around, I mean, I hang around, wait, I stay in the small room for a few more minutes watching this chick dance until my window closes again. I did pay for the last few minutes, might as well enjoy the eye candy a little longer.

And, now for my grand exit. As I leave my private booth, there's a small crowd of people looking, walking by giving glaring glances, while others are exiting the building. I spot the guys I came in with, who shall remain nameless and I start making my way over towards the exit area as well. But I can already see that look in their eyes. It's just a look but you know something is up look.

"What?" I say as I look around and back towards the booth area. It's then that I notice from the outside of the booths, each room is only separated by a small wooden panel and a plywood door, cheaply made I might add, that anyone within a three block radius could probably hear through, especially, if some guy is in one, not whispering, but yelling, "Take off your shoes!" Needless to say, I hit that exit door quicker and faster than I ever hit the ring ropes.

*What?*

130

# ◅ I'm No Angel ◈

*Some names have been changed to protect the innocent*

Yeah, I've done a lot of crazy things during my lifetime. I've always tried to do the right things or things that would make others happy, but sometimes I've just gone off the rails and have done some things that made me pretty happy too. And, well if they didn't make me happy, the best way to describe it is Bobby Blaze Entertainment, as mentioned earlier. If nothing else these few things ended up making for a good story or two. So, I guess you could say I'm no angel.

One time my now ex, but then wife, Carolyn and I were having trouble in our marriage and had been arguing. It's crazy when all you do is travel then come home and just want to relax and or chill out with your family. One of these times we had a really big blow out right before I had to go and do a three day loop down in the Atlanta area. I remember the loop and this particular time period well. I was to fly into Atlanta, Georgia to do a show there that night, then I had to go up to Rome, Georgia the second night before finishing up on the third day in Chattanooga, Tennessee. I was supposed to drive back to Atlanta, then fly home, but I rebooked my flight to fly back home from Chattanooga to HTS, Huntington, Tri-State Airport with a small layover in Charlotte, North Carolina. I had changed my ticket to fly back home right before the show started on that last night because I had to get back home to my baby. Plus, I had to straighten another matter out asap. I was crazy for her and as we spoke right before the show started, I just knew we had worked things out. I was coming home to her. Maybe?

But, let me back up. Before I flew out to start the loop I had a night from crazy hell. This is where "you can't make this kind of stuff up" comes in. I had my bags packed and was ready to be dropped off at the airport early the next morning when hell night was to begin. Carolyn had decided to go for a little family ride, so she, our boys, and I all got into my SUV for what I thought was a "family ride." I should have known something was up when she requested that she drive. So we end up at a certain person's house and that's where things start to get a little crazy. I'm innocent mind

131

you. Read into that what you will. Anyway, the person, whose house we arrived at was that of a girl who I was supposedly sleeping with. We will call her Barbie. I wasn't. It was all fun and games up until now. I assure you my dear reader nothing had happened other than some flirting and a friendship between two people who probably shouldn't have been so friendly with each other. Anyway, we, meaning, Carolyn, Barbie, and I were sitting there talking as we both assured my wife that nothing was going on between us. There really hadn't been at this time. I can be a bastard at times, but this one time I wasn't. I was being loyal to my wife. She was the love of my life, and even though I came close to jeopardizing that a couple of times, this being one, I was loyal. The other woman was a friend who I had met at the gym and was going through a divorce. I wasn't quite at the divorce stage yet, but it was rapidly moving across the horizon at this time period. Anyway, I was just trying to be the guy friend lending some male support and guy advice. It appears current wives, and angry ex-husbands don't like it when you're trying to play Mr. Nice guy. But, as you know with me, it's always, "And one thing leads to another." Mind you I have an early morning flight and it's getting to be about ten o'clock in the evening when the following took place.

Somewhere in the conversation, my wife had said she was going check on the kids, they were playing in the other room with my lady friend's kid, so they weren't around any arguing or adult conversation, thank goodness. Well Barbie and I continued to talk without realizing quite a few minutes had passed. I am seriously just chilling out, being all cool and stuff, thinking, it's all going to be okay while talking to this other lady and that I just didn't want to make this more than what it was. We could be friends, but obviously, due to the current situation, we couldn't be more than that at this point in our lives. I believed that too. I really did. The next thing I hear is the sound of a horn honking, and it just seems to be getting louder and louder and going on and on before I realize that's it's the horn on my SUV going off. I go to the front door as the horn continues to blast away, I think, well I guess it's time for me to go. Carolyn had other ideas. I wasn't going to be riding home with her that night. I see her leaving with my two kids; both boys were young at the time, leaving my ass there standing on the front porch alone, except for my two travel bags which had been thrown out into the front lawn. I am standing there dumbfounded. So, I walk out into the yard and pick up my travel bags, one had a couple of changes of clothes in it along with personal items, and the other had close to a thousand dollars' worth of wrestling gear inside of it. I had two pairs of boots, several different wrestling singlets and trunks along with other assorted things such as knee pads, extra socks, and a few other gimmicks that I always traveled with.

Meanwhile, Barbie is standing in her front doorway just looking at me like, WTF? So, I calmly picked up my bags and asked her to give me a ride home. I then placed my bags on her front porch and went inside to discuss whether she was going to give me a ride home or not. I tried calling my wife on her cell phone just to try to reason with her as to what the hell just happened, but she didn't pick up. Of course not! Anyway, I just told Barbie to take me on up to the airport, as we weren't too far from it anyway, and I would just get a rental and go on home myself. I told her I can take myself home and work this out, and if things get too crazy, yeah right, as they were about to, I'd just come back and hang out at the airport until my flight. Well, when I went back out front, my bags were missing. Gone! I know I had just set them on the front porch, and I hadn't been inside the house for more than a few minutes. So what the hell happened to my bags? I've got a flight to catch in just a few hours and now my gear is missing.

I go back in, and now I'm really starting to try and grasp just what has happened. I called the cell phone. Of course it went straight to voice mail. I start calling my home number and after several tries Carolyn picks up the phone. Good to know she and the boys are at least home safe. But now the bigger question is, if she is home, who took my bags? I thought maybe she had doubled back and took them as a mean and cruel joke as if just leaving me here wasn't enough. You women can be treacherous bitches when someone messes with your man. But, when she picked up the home phone there was no way she had time to double back and then be home. That meant someone else had stolen my gear from the front porch. Now I go back in, call the police and have to make a report because there were a lot of valuable belongings in those bags. Talking to Barbie, again, we were only friends people, I'm telling her I'll just go to the airport, get a rental car, go home, pack another bag, and fly out as planned in the morning. I told her I was going to do this just as soon as the police get here and I file the report. Did I mention it's getting late and I have to fly out on the first flight to Charlotte to make my connection to Atlanta early in the morning? So the police come, and as I'm filling out a report, Barbie comes out and says she knows where my stuff is. My wife, who had at least spoken to me over the phone by now and because I questioned her about my bags, of which she had no clue or idea other than she threw them out when she left my ass there, had called back and spoken to Barbie. She said that Barbie's ex had called her to brag about what he had done with my bags.

So, at this point she's at least concerned about my bags, as she knows my livelihood is in them, and that is equal to a pay check. Think Henry Hill yelling at Karen in *GoodFellas* about this time, as it seems to be all that I have left is what's in those bags to make the towns and to make money. Wrestling gear, not drugs were in them, but that was everything I had in order to make a living.

As I said my ex had received a call from Barbie's ex, who apparently had been down the street and saw her toss my bags, and when I went in to make my first calls to my wife on her cell, snuck up to his ex–wife's house. He had been parked over the hill watching all of this as it unfolded, because in his head, I was the one responsible for his divorce. I wasn't! Anyway, when he saw me go back in, he grabbed the bags and threw them over a hill out behind his house. He then called my wife to brag about what he had done. Carolyn then called over to Barbie's house to tell me where my bags were. So, in mid report to the police, Barbie comes out and says the bags are over the hill somewhere in the woods. The policeman, who must have thought we were all nuts, goes out with his flashlight with me and Barbie and we search through the woods, and low and behold, there are my bags about thirty feet down an embankment out behind her house. Well fuck me!

So anyway, I got down over the hill, got my bags and Barbie ended up taking me to the airport where I picked up a rental car. I then went home to an empty house as Carolyn had gone over to stay at her dad's house before I got back home. So, bags packed in the rental, I'm in my own home, and just as I'm about to try to fall asleep I hear the front door open. Now what? Well, it's Carolyn, and she is storming through the house because she just knew I had, "That other woman in there," but I didn't. I told you I was at least trying to be innocent in all of this. I told her about the rental, and that was how I got home.

I really needed to get some sleep or I was heading on up to the airport and would sleep in the car, fuck all this craziness. She's now convinced that nothing is going on, at least for now, and leaves so I can get some sleep. I may have gotten two to three hours in before I had to catch my flight. You do remember I had a flight to catch and towns to make in all this mess, right?

Early the next morning I make my flights and make it to Atlanta to start the loop. I couldn't even tell you who I wrestled each night. I remember telling a couple of the boys about my crazy hell night and I don't even think they believed me. After each show, I stayed self-medicated and pretty much to myself in my room until it was time to make it to each town. Again, I'm no angel, but other than trying to call home as often as I could during those three days, I wasn't getting much rest so I had to find something to get into, and I did, and as you know by now, one thing just leads to another.

I remember the last phone call from the arena in Chattanooga to Carolyn. I had told her I had changed my flights and would be earlier than expect by a couple of hours and to meet me at the airport with my SUV and my boys. After my match that night, again, no idea who I worked with or much about the card, I was going to get some rest, get on that early flight and head back home. That's where things got blurry again. My Bad!

I don't recall how I got from my hotel to the airport the following morning, but I do recall waking up in Charlotte. I went straight to the bar in between flights for some more self-medication before I had to make my connecting flight home. I was on a first name basis with the bartender there. "Hi Jan," if you're reading this, thanks for the early morning Long Island Iced Teas. Gulp!

Now, I'm on the runway, all buckled in, feeling no pain and ready to make it home. The next thing I hear is the laughter of two little old ladies setting across the aisle from me. It was a small prop plane and their laughter was louder than the engine. I woke up with spit and drool running down my chin, rubbing my eyes, and saying, "That sure was a short flight." The ladies along with the flight attendant and a couple of others sitting nearby just smiled and laughed a little more as I attempted to wipe my face and collect my thoughts. "Honey, we haven't even left Charlotte yet. There's been a weather delay and we are number nine in line waiting for clearance for takeoff. You've been asleep for about thirty minutes." At least that's what I think the stewardess said. Ha-ha! What else could I do except sit there and laugh at myself? So, I made a few jokes to the ladies across from me and tried to act like I wasn't embarrassed, don't worry, I wasn't. It was just funny. My crazy hell night had turned into a crazy hell week at this point, because it seemed to just go on and on and on.

Fast asleep again after actual take off, yeah, I made sure we left the ground. I again heard a female voice as it was that of the stewardess saying, "Sir, sir, please wake up we have landed safely at Huntington Tri-State Airport and we really need you get off the plane. All the other passengers have exited." I thanked her, exited the plane and made my way to baggage claim.

Now, keep in mind, I thought all things were fine and dandy back home. Also keep in mind I had changed my flight so I could get back home a couple of hours ahead of time to see my wife. I used the pay phone; does anyone remember using one of them? Anyway, I used my pre-paid calling card, called home and told Carolyn I was at the airport. She said she would be on her way. Little did I know. At the time, we only lived about a twenty minute drive from the airport, depending on traffic, so I went outside to wait for her. Oh, yeah, keep in mind; I'm still self-medicated as I had a couple of more shots once I got my bags. Might as well keep this buzz going, right?

I lay my bags down, you remember them don't you? Yeah, they're the same ones that have been packed, tossed from a SUV, thrown over a hill, found, repacked, put in a rental car, taken on the road, from airport to airport, hotel to hotel, and rental car to rental car, to now actually feeling pretty comfortable as I really needed to lie down for a minute. This has been one crazy hell week. So, I laid my bags out behind some bushes, laid my head down for what I thought would only be about twenty minutes and passed out again. Kids, don't try this at your local airport, especially in today's security environment. This was pre 911.

The next voice I heard was one that will be forever in my mind. "Robert! Robert! Wake up!" Yep, it was Carolyn. Only my mom, Carolyn, and a couple of close friends ever called me Robert, and in the tone I was hearing it, well you can imagine. Of course I tried to play it off, "Oh hey baby. How are you? You been alright? I sure am glad to see you." Then I looked at my watch, and saw that another two hours had passed. What? Yep, she had purposely waited a couple of hours to come and get me. "Just get your bags and get in, so we can go home." Rut Ro! She's driving again, thankfully, this time she takes me to our house. Let's just say it was a quiet ride home that day. I don't blame her for picking me up late; she had every right to still be mad. Besides, I needed the sleep. I was just glad this trip was over. I was glad this crazy night that had ended up going on for days was finally over and that I was home where I belonged.

Well, like I said, I'm no angel. We really tried to make things work, but in the end life is full of twist and turns. We had a good run together. She said it was a funny story and that I should include it as we can laugh about it now, but it wasn't so funny back then. Like I said, with me, one thing just leads to another.

## ❧ Dyin' an a Smilin' ❧

"I was talking with a friend of mine, said a woman had hurt his pride," wait, that's the lyrics to a Tom Petty song, anyway...I was talking to a friend of mine, and it could have been any number of only a few guys or friends who I talk to, so I won't mention names. Anyway that's not the important thing; the story is what's important, which I'll get to in a second. My friends, or the guys that know me, know how to take what I say, the way I mean it, depending on how I say it, the way it's meant. It can be taken quite literally, it can be taken seriously, or usually in a laughing sardonic way. There's usually no guess work involved.

So, we're sitting around talking and a couple of my favorite subjects come into the conversation, women and food. Well, the conversation was actually about religion, death, and the great beyond, so how women and food came into the conversation is a bit on the far side even for me, but hell, my mind often drifts off into any number of places during a conversation, so maybe I brought it up, I don't know. But anyway, after a few laughs and a good time I thought on this great theological talk a little later on. During our talk we were talking dying doing something you like or loved doing as opposed to some other tragic way. Well, as I said, I thought a great deal about this and have come to this conclusion.

I hope the fuck I die with a stripper on one side of me, the smell of a greasy cheeseburger on my breath and a smile on my face. That way, when people start their coffin talk, you know, standing there talking about the dearly departed over the casket, they'll at least have something good to talk about over me. I know they will, and you know they will too. Hell, they'll talk about you too. It seems everyone has someone doing the usual coffin talk. I'm not so sure what our fascination with talking about dead people is, but we all do it, "Ya know Bubba, well I was just talkin' to him down at the bait store the other day," or "Ya know he still owes me ten dollars from last year's football pool, I guess I'll never see that." Insert your own witty standing by the casket whispered saying here. Just make sure you have a laugh when you do.

Now there was a time when I used to eat a little better, I dare say I used to eat very healthy. I used to always do some sort of exercise. I've done everything from basketball to running, and weight lifting. That's no longer the case so the chances of finding me pinned down under a squat rack or bench press are slim and the chances of finding me face down after going jogging or running are even slimmer. If

138

they say that he was found dead from running, please find out who was chasing me. So when people start whispering, talking, or laughing about a funny story, they'll say, "Well you know they found him lying in bed with a stripper don't ya? Hell, he had a Big Mac box crunched up under his back. You know that couldn't have been comfortable. But ya know what? He had a big ol' smile on his face when he died. The mortician said all he had to do was apply a little makeup and comb back his hair because there was no way he could have improved that smile on his face." Then you can laugh and say, "At least he was doing something he loved when he died." Yep, I want to be a smilin' when I die.

## ☙ Eleven ☙

*"Always go to other peoples funerals; otherwise they won't come to yours."—Yogi Berra*

## ☙ To Those Who Moved On 2.0 ☙

Speaking of dying, once again I find myself writing about many of the professional wrestlers that have left us way too soon. I'm not sure there's such a thing as a timely death, but so many professional wrestlers seem to die at an early age. Every time a wrestler dies, I get personal phone calls, text, and my social media links all blow up about who died and if I knew them or had wrestled them. It always reminds me just how little time we all have on this planet as well as reminding me of my own mortality. "No one here gets out alive." That's a shoot.

By the time you read this, sadly more may have also passed away. I just hope I'm not one of them. Like I told my brother, "I'm just trying to outlive a few more people, including myself." I'll be using only stage or ring names for each person that I pay my respects to in this section. Again, you can always check the internet to find out just how many pro wrestlers have died in the last couple of years, and of course you can find out their real names there. As for me, I try to remember people the way I knew them and by the name I called them. I personally knew or worked in the ring or shared a locker room at one time or another with many of the departed who I'll mention. There are a couple of guys who, like most of you, I only knew as a fan of the sport. I don't want to leave anyone out but, if I forget someone, I apologize in advance. I'm not going to make up some story like I knew some of these guys personally if I didn't. If I don't actually have a story to tell, I won't. I'll just make mention of the person and keep on moving through my thoughts. Again, I'll throw a story in from time to time between the names to keep the story going and not make it so somber.

I don't really do funerals. Sometimes I go to a viewing for a quick visit, and by quick, I mean, I may or may not sign the visitor book, make a quick pass by the coffin, and try to get out of there before I have to speak to anyone. With that said, just like in the chapter, "Just Passing Through" in my last book, to me, adding this chapter is a way for me to honor the men and women who gave or dedicated their life to the professional wrestling business, and a way that I hope that if someone is reading what I wrote or said, then they will remember something good or special about a person, and they will live on in our memories. Once again, the stories I will share are without judgment and will be only of the good memories that I have about each person that I make mention of. I'll also only be writing about each person as to how they were to me and around me. Most wrestlers were mere acquaintances as that's just the nature of our business. Some I got to know better than others, but either way, I'm honored to have met so many great talents in the wrestling business during the course of my life.

Many more talents have passed away since 2013 when, *Pin Me Pay Me* was published. There's an even longer listing in the story called "just passing through."

Verne Gagne. The man was a true legend in the professional wrestling business. I've heard tons of Verne stories from the boys who knew and worked for him, but I never met him. I did enjoy his AWA wrestling shows back in the day and thought he was one of the true champions in our sport.

Nick Bockwinkle was a great champion. There are not enough good things I could say about the way he carried himself as the AWA World Heavyweight Champion. I never had the pleasure of meeting him, but I did enjoy his matches. I certainly respected him as a world champion. I got to see him wrestle from time to time because the old Memphis videos showed some of his matches on a regular basis. A few years later we would get to see the AWA regularly in my area. I always liked how he was like a ring general in his matches. It was obvious that he was a very sound technician in the ring, but if and when he "cheated" or needed to take a shortcut or two to win a match he was very tactful in the way he did it. I didn't know it then, but what I was watching was the way he used or had great ring psychology during those matches. As I said, he was a great wrestler and a very worthy champion.

I never met Maddog Vachon, another AWA mainstay and star. Billy Robinson was a great shooter and a tough performer who had some phenomenal ring work back in the day, but I never met him. I've seen footage and heard stories about how legit he was. I would have loved to have seen him work in his prime. I never met Lord James Blears and don't remember seeing him wrestle or manage too much even when I was younger. Surprisingly, as much as I was around the WWF and up in Canada back in the day, I never met "Iron" Mike Sharpe. I always thought he had really good matches with just about everyone he stepped into the ring with. Recently WWE Hall of Famer Blackjack Mulligan passed away. I never met him personally, but I heard many stories about how tough he was in and outside the ring. I remember seeing him wrestle and always thought that he could really move well for a big man. May he rest in peace.

A couple of female wrestling legends also passed away recently. Cora Combs was from Kentucky and one of the first female wrestlers I got to see wrestle as a young boy. I would watch, "Lady Satan" in the days of the old ICW. She would always battle a beautiful young lady wrestler named Debbie Combs. Debbie, as my friends and I would soon all find out was her daughter. Cora held many championships including the NWA United States Woman's Championship on four different occasions.

Mae Young was an early pioneer in women's professional wrestling. Unless you're really old you will probably remember her most from still getting in the ring and performing with the WWE, but she was the first NWA United States Champion and wrestled in nine different decades. I remember her winning the Miss Royal Rumble back in the early 2000's, but what was more impressive was that she was still taking bumps when she had to have been up in her 80's. She was inducted into the WWE Hall Of Fame in 2008 and rightfully so.

Chyna, the big strong body building female bodyguard, enforcer, and wrestler sadly passed away recently as I was finishing up this book. She wasn't just eye candy standing at the side of the ring. She often competed with the men in the

Attitude Era of the WWF. For political reasons, who knows if she will ever be inducted into their HOF, but she was the first women to enter the yearly Royal Rumble and also was the first and only lady to hold the WWE Intercontinental Championship belt. She also graced the covers of several well know magazines including, *Playboy*.

Famous Japanese star, Hayabusa passed away while I was finishing up this chapter of the book. I met him several times while touring Japan for Michinoku Pro Wrestling. He, along with a couple of other Japanese stars from Frontier Martial Arts Wrestling (FMW) came over and worked several shows while I was there. I was actually involved in a couple of six-man tag matches where he joined forces with The Great Sasuke and Gran Hamada going against myself and whoever the office put me with on the heel side. I remember him being very smooth in the ring, but we didn't talk or have much to say to each other outside of the ring. Still, it's sad to see a guy I knew from around the world passing away, even if I just knew him briefly.

We lost a couple of luchador stars from Mexico in recent years as well. I knew Hector Garza and was around him a lot when I was in WCW. I would speak to him at catering and got to enjoy many of his matches during our time together there, but I really never got to know him on a personal level. He seemed like a nice enough guy but our relationship was strictly a professional one. Perro Aguayo Jr died in an in ring incident. I watched the video of his in ring death several times and all I can provide is my opinion on it. To me, he already looked dead before the follow up move was performed on him. It's quite sad to watch his motionless body in the ring. I think his death was possibly the result of a prior injury that had been neglected or ignored in order to get in the ring and perform. That's what wrestlers love doing, working and performing no matter the injuries or how bad our bodies may hurt at times.

## ⊷ Buddy Landel ❧

*"Yeah I said it!"*

I first met Buddy Landel way back in 1988 during my rookie year in professional wrestling. We were scheduled to appear on the same show in Pikeville, Kentucky. I worked in the third match on the card that was part of a big Christmas show. Buddy was scheduled to work the main event against Lazor Tron and "Boogie Woogie Man" Jimmy Valiant. I'm not sure who was supposed to be Buddy's tag partner that day, but his partner no-showed. As the matches moved along and his partner still hadn't shown up, Buddy spoke up and said, "Put that young boy right there in with me. We'll still have a tag match and everything will be fine." And, that's what the promoter did. He teamed me and Buddy together to work in the main event. My very first main event I might add. Plus, I got an extra ten dollars to go back out to work again, which brought my pay for the night up to forty-five dollars. Hey, that's not bad considering I still hadn't even had proper and professional training at the time. It was during this match as I stood on the ring apron that I realized just how much of a work the wrestling business was, and it also smartened me up to the fact that I had a long way to go and needed lots more professional training.

Fast forward several years to my time in Smoky Mountain Wrestling as that would be the next time that I would run into Buddy and eventually work a program with him over the SMW Heavyweight Title. Many probably know about or have heard about how Buddy was destined to become the NWA World Heavyweight Champion by now, so I'll spare you the details. Like he told me, that was one very costly and expensive nap.

When Buddy was on, there was none better. There were also times when Buddy was off. I'm not going knock him for the times he was off, as many know the demons Buddy battled, as many of us in this business have as well. There were times when I butted heads with Buddy, but they were usually quickly resolved. One such time that comes to mind was the one night I had to short-arm scissor him in Morristown, Tennessee. It was a two out of three falls match. In order to get his mind on what match it was (second fall, with me going over) I had to hook him and take him down.

I held him until he collected himself and got back on track. I didn't do it to hurt him or embarrass him. I did it for the fans, for his best interest, and for the match. I didn't want him getting in trouble for screwing something up, um, like a finish. He realized I was right as I locked on the hold and told him to basically get his head out of his ass. He did, and the match continued. That's just a small example of him being off. Those times were few and far between when I was working my program with Ol' Budro. Another night Sandy Scott came to Buddy and told him to go out and have a good match with me. He told Buddy that there was no excuse as to why he couldn't have a solid match. Buddy being Buddy, had been breezing through some easy matches on the loop that week.

He had a little bit of bad heat going on at the time with the office and the boys. Well, that night, Buddy and I tore the house down in the main event. It wasn't a five star match, but the few hundred people who were there for the house show sure got one heck of a match from us on that night. That was a night when Buddy was on.

Buddy could work and proved it many times over throughout his career. He had an excellent match with Shawn Michaels in Knoxville, Tennessee on the Super Bowl of Wrestling along with so many other good matches with some of the top stars from the UWF, NWA, and SMW. As I said, Buddy could work when he decided to work.

My favorite match with Buddy took place in my hometown for the SMW Heavyweight Title. We had already had a big match in Johnson City, Tennessee about ten days prior to working in Ashland. I had dropped the belt to him on the show in Freedom Hall. The TV taping hadn't been played yet in this area and back then the closest cable company that aired SMW was about thirty miles from Ashland. I wasn't so sure whether the hometown people knew or didn't know that I had already lost the title. I did know that we had fans who followed us from towns as far away as three to four hours to the house shows. I spoke to Buddy about what to do as the posters all had me listed as the champion in a title defense against, "The Nature Boy" Buddy Landel. So, being in my hometown, part owner of the promotion, CPW, that had run here prior to bringing in SMW, I wanted to make sure that we didn't get accused of false advertising, and I didn't want to lose any good heat that was already built up between Buddy and me. The town was important to me, as the promoter, as a talent, and because it was my home town. I knew that we would get a good reaction either way. Buddy had a brief confrontation two months prior when a fan tried to interfere in our match. Buddy knocked the guy out as he climbed up on the ring apron. I then grabbed Buddy and he started saying, "Beat me up Bobby. Stay on me. Don't let up." I did, too. I had to. The fans had just seen a shoot, so I had to work extra stiff and stayed on him until the finish. So, it was easy to get heat for this return match, as everyone knew Buddy was a real heel and I was a solid face. The problem for me was, again, I thought maybe I should go out with the belt and drop it to him again. But, I also knew we had to do what was best for business.

Once I ran a couple ideas by Buddy, he said he would think about it. He actually said he would "pray" about it. I told Sandy Scott that I really didn't know what we were going to do, but I would do what was best for the business. At the time Ashland was drawing pretty well, so I didn't want to kill the town off with a poor match or poor booking decision over the finish. Sandy said that we should work it out and no matter who went to the ring with the belt; Buddy had to leave with it.

Of course I already knew that and had no problem with it, it's just a tricky situation where you always want the fans to not only enjoy all the matches, but you want them to especially remember yours as you're the advertised champ and it's your home town. So, about five minutes before the match Buddy thinks he should carry the belt to the ring and throws out a finish that we both agree on.

When we began the match, Buddy was on. We proceeded to have a real solid and entertaining match. The fans were into it. It was just a classic old school match and both of us worked our asses off. In the finish, I had Buddy in the corner and as he reached into his tights to get his gimmick, a chain, out of them, I kicked him. He dropped the chain. Referee Mark Curtis was busy backing Buddy up and I grabbed the gimmick. Turning Buddy into the turnbuckle, I let him have it, a solid shot to the head with the chain wrapped around my hand, and he dropped like a bag of dirt to the mat. I quickly covered him for the pin and the win. "And, once again, your new Smoky Mountain Heavyweight Champion, Bobby Blaze!" came over the speakers as my music hit in the background... But this match wasn't quite over yet. As Mark Curtis raised my hand he saw the gimmick and immediately took the gimmick out of my hand and also tried to take the belt. Meanwhile, Buddy was laying right there in the middle of the ring flat on his back. The decision was reversed and Buddy was declared the winner. I then went over and dropped the belt right across Buddy's body as he was "out." The fans popped on both finishes when I went over, and when I dropped the title on him. As I said, Buddy was on that night, and he was a true professional about the finish.

When I reached the back, Sandy asked me who came up with the finish. I thought maybe he was hot about it, and I said Buddy did, but I also agreed to it. Sandy said, "Kid that was a great finish for you. You just got over in your home town. You left the champ lying in the middle of the ring, with the title across his body. And, you two had a hell of a match, you should be proud." I was proud, the office was happy, the fans were happy, and both Buddy and I had done the right thing by having him go out as the champ, and me "winning" the title in my town, only to throw in a swerve to keep the belt on Buddy. That was a hell of a finish you called Buddy. Thank you! That is why this is one of my favorite matches with Buddy. Buddy you were a top talent and it was an honor to share the ring with you. RIP Buddy Landel. Thanks for the memories.

## ✥ And the List Goes On ✥

You want more? You got it. Again, there's more to add to the list of deceased wrestlers. The list is forever growing as no man goes undefeated against Father Time. He makes us all tap out at some point.

Buddy Wayne used to work and promote in the old Memphis territory. I remember seeing him on Saturday mornings as a wrestler, but from my understanding he made a lot more money learning the promotional part of wrestling and did quite well for himself promoting towns that the old Memphis territory used to run regularly. Another wrestler turned promoter was Steve Rickard. Many may not be familiar with Steve as he promoted out of New Zealand. I had heard his name for years, but it wasn't until I became good friends with promoter and referee Frank Shanly from New Zealand. Frank shared many exciting stories about Steve and about his promotion and the shows that took place in New Zealand.

One international star I did meet was Drew McDonald. I met Drew while I was on a tour in South Africa. He and a German wrestler were walking along the beach when Ron Starr and I ran into him. Ron knew him from working with him in another territory. I think they had been in Stampede Wrestling in Calgary together. He was there on tour with another wrestling promoter at the time I was there. We ended up having a few drinks together later that night in Cape Town. I didn't see Drew again until I saw him one more time while I was touring England. He was a big strong Scottish wrestler who was well known throughout the UK.

As I have made mention of, I grew up watching the old Memphis videos. "The Fabulous One" Jackie Fargo competed in Memphis and many Southeastern regional promotions, as well as for the National Wrestling Alliance during the 1950s, 1960s and 1970s. I got to see Jackie Fargo wrestle quite often on TV on Saturday mornings during the seventies. Jackie was a huge influence on many younger stars. He was a huge influence and mentor to Jerry "The King" Lawler. He did a strut in the ring that has many times been imitated but never duplicated and was and still is famously known as, "The Fargo Strut." I never got to see him wrestle live or meet him in person. "Fantastic" Bobby Fulton has shared many stories with me through the years about Jackie, so it kind of seems like I did know him a little bit. "Fabulous" Jackie Fargo was larger than life and a true wrestling legend.

Speaking of Bobby Fulton, many may remember him as being one half of the world famous, "Fantastics." Bobby and I have been friends for over twenty years. Recently his partner, Tommy Rogers passed away. I was rather blown away when I heard the news. I wrestled Tommy back when I was in Florida for a promotion called, "Sun Coast Pro Wrestling." I would often run into Tommy either at the gym or on the local shows in the area. He was one of the first people to tell me to call Cornette. Through Tommy I got to eventually meet Bobby. It was through working for Bobby that I eventually got the call-back from Cornette and my tryout for SMW. Tommy was a tremendously talented wrestler. He and Bobby worked on sold out shows in Dallas for World Class Championship Wrestling and worked in legendary territories like the UWF, Memphis, and The NWA in the Carolinas, and were also super stars in Japan for years.

Ron Wright was a mainstay in East Tennessee both as a wrestler and as a manager. He was a legendary heel who I only got to meet on the tail end of his career while he was managing, "The Dirty White Boy" Tony Anthony during my run in SMW. It's been said, that no other wrestler in the Knoxville area had his ability to tell and help get over a storyline or get as much crowd heat as Ron Wright. The Knoxville News said, "Fans never felt cheated when Mr. Wright was in the ring or on television."

Archie "The Mongolian Stomper" Gouldie had a look that would scare the daylights out of anyone who saw his growling, grimacing face. I know he scared me the first time I saw him on TV on the old Memphis territory recordings when I was a kid. I met him several years later when he was working on house shows for SMW. He always was in fantastic shape and could move well for a man of his size.

He seemed quite nice and friendly around me, but other than casual conversations with me and me always addressing him with a very deserving and respectful, "Yes sir," we had limited contact with each other in the ring except maybe the occasional battle royal, but he had that same scary demeanor about him that I remembered as a kid, so I always made sure to keep my distance and to be respectful.

Gypsy Joe was another great wrestler who passed away as I was trying to complete this book. I thought I'd better add him in quick as this chapter just seems to keep getting longer, quicker and quicker. It's just a matter of time before some other wrestler dies as it seems to be happening on a monthly if not weekly basis. I've got to get this thing published. I first saw him wrestle on the old TV tapings that came out of Oak Hill, West Virginia when I was a kid, and later on the recordings that came out of Memphis. I also saw him wrestle in person way back in 1976 in Ashland. He was using the ring name Gene Madrid back then. Even though I never met him I later heard a few stories about him from

Goldie Rogers when Goldie was a rookie in 76'. Goldie referred to him as Gypsy but said he remembered him as Gene Madrid. Goldie said he had taken him under his wing for about six months and he had learned a few lessons from him. Gypsy Joe had a legendary career. He was well known throughout the Tennessee area to Japan and all points in between. He was a known brawler who had a toughness to him and was also known for his hardcore style of wrestling.

Chuck Conley was born in Paintsville, Kentucky, but was raised in my hometown of Ashland. He was well known and respected throughout the sixties and seventies during his wrestling heyday. Sadly, he passed away during the summer that my last book was coming out and it was in the editing stage so I couldn't add him to my list of those who were, "Just passing through." I had known Chuck since I was a young boy as I was a fan of, "The Scufflin' Hillbillies" along with his partner Rip Collins. Rip passed away in 1993. Chuck was a former Marine and actually got involved in professional wrestling while still in the Marines. He was a big strong man back in the day. I'll always remember him referring to me or calling me, "Kid." In return, I always called him, "Old timer." He and I really liked that we had a special bond with each other in that he could call me a kid and I could call him an old timer. We both understood and found honor in the fact that we both meant it with the utmost respect for one another. I remember him coming to some local shows back in the nineties when I was running shows and he still had a big chest and big strong arms even then, and he would have been in his sixties by this time. One night he even took a bump while he was using a cane to get around. The use of the cane was a shoot. On this night, Chuck was doing an interview when manager, "Classy" Roy Bass kicked it out from under him. It was a solid bump on a hardwood floor and it was picture perfect when he took it. It really generated some good in house heat for that night's house show. Chuck ended up being my "second" or in my corner that night for the main event. It ended up turning out great as he got to relive some of that glory that we all miss from being in the ring from time to time. I really liked Chuck and always tried visiting him whenever I could, either with my brother or another good friend of mine who had known him a long time. Chuck was good people as we sometimes say here in Eastern Kentucky. He was just an all-around good guy.

Charlie Fulton has also passed away as I am near completion of this book. I met Charlie at, "The Monster Factory" as that was the first place I went when I was trying to break into the business. I had received a call back from them prior to hearing back from Malenko's. Of course I ended up deciding to head south to sunny Florida instead of New Jersey. Charlie returned my call and we scheduled a day for me to come up for a tryout. Charlie was the man in the ring with me when I took my first bump. He had me do a couple of drills, like running the ropes, doing a couple of forward rolls and then eventually taking a back bump. I didn't see him again until I saw him years later on an independent show up in Ohio. I greeted him with a handshake and introduced myself, but never mentioned the Monster Factory tryout. He was very cordial and of course professional. I know a lot of guys who he helped out as well as guys he had helped get over on their way to stardom. He was a known journeyman and unsung hero in the wrestling business.

Mabel also known as Viscera, Duke Myers, Hack Myers, Reid Flair, Axl Rotten and Sean O'Haire along with Matt "Doink" Borne all have died in the last couple of years. I only met Sean briefly when he and I were in WCW together for a short time. I didn't meet or know Duke Myers, but felt like I did know him some as Goldie Rogers and Eddie Watts told me many funny stories about him when they all worked in the Stampede territory together. I did meet, "The Original Doink" several times through the years. It still drives me crazy when some of these idiots on independent shows either try to promote a "Doink" on their show or then try to do his gimmick in the ring. Hey people it's 2016, the guy, and the gimmick for that matter, is dead.

ECW Original Balls Mahoney, dead! I knew him when he was running around SMW as Boo Bradley. He really hit his stride, I guess because he fit in better when he worked for ECW. We always got along together just fine whether it was back when we worked regularly for SMW or when we would see each other on some independent show. We pulled a big rib together one night while working for Cleveland All-Pro

Wrestling. We saw each other coming into the building about the same time and no one saw us out in the parking lot as we greeted each other. We had a few laughs together and caught up on some old times for a few minutes. Wrestlers are supposed to be at the show at least one hour before show time. Well Balls and I must have been real early for whatever reason. So I get this idea to maybe "have a real fight" in the dressing room when he does get inside later on. I set the first hook into my friend JT Lightning by telling him that Balls and I had some legitimate heat with each other. I let him know that something good was about to take place but to just play it straight when all the boys came into the locker room. I then waited until all the faces were in the locker room and I cut into JT for booking Balls and me on the same show. I told him that there was serious heat between us and I wished I had known he had booked him. I think JT may have even said he was sorry as he had no idea, so the hook was set in front of the boys as well. About twenty minutes goes by and in comes Balls screaming my name saying he just heard that I was over in the baby face locker room. I'm sitting on a couch trying to get up as I start cussing him back but he is already on top of me. We start hitting each other from a tied up position, so even though we are hitting each other hard and the punches were real, they were being thrown from short distances as we were still wrestling around some and kind of tied up with each other so we really weren't hurting each other as we fought. As we went down to the floor from the couch it looked like a straight shoot.

We got everyone's attention as the boys really bought into the yelling, screaming, punches and wrestling until, as we were tied up and both of us started laughing out loud as we were trying to untangle our bodies. It was a pretty good rib and everyone was relieved to find out we really didn't hate each other nor did we have heat between us. Everyone eventually had a good laugh about it as we shook hands and had a good laugh ourselves. Good match Balls.

I'm not sure if anyone was shocked with the passing of, "The Ultimate Warrior," or if they thought it was a cruel joke when they heard it. There's nothing I can really say about Warrior that you probably don't already know. I never met him personally, although I did see him in person several times on shows that I had attended. I do know that while watching *WrestleMania XXX* my friend told me that he didn't look good and then the next night on Monday Night Raw, another person pointed out that he just didn't look good. I'm not sure what was going on, but something didn't seem quite right about his appearance. With that said, we all know what happened next and that's a sad reality of the wrestling world. The good thing was that he got to make one big final appearance and get the glory that he was due taking his place in the WWE Hall of Fame.

## ✧ Roddy Piper ✧

*Hot Rod*

"I have come here to kick ass and chew bubblegum...and I'm all out of bubblegum."

As many people as may have been shocked and saddened at the untimely death of The Warrior, it's my opinion that even more were shocked when the announcement was made that wrestling legend and all-time great "Rowdy" Roddy Piper died. Roddy Piper was an ICON in professional wrestling. He was probably the greatest villain in the history of pro wrestling. "Rowdy," "Hot Rod" or just Piper, no matter what one called him was one of the most gifted wrestlers to ever grace the ring. He could brawl, as he was tough, he could box, wrestle, or fight. He could talk as he was intelligent and quick witted, and he could back it all up. There's not enough I could say about him that everyone doesn't already know. So, I'll share something about Piper that many may not know. I wrestled him! I wrestled him in Huntington, West Virginia for the WWF Super Stars of Wrestling show.

I had just finished up working my first tour in Canada out in the Maritimes back in 1991. I heard WWF was going to be in my area as I had at the time just come back to Ashland. A couple of my friends from Malenko's told me they had worked some TV spots for them when they had come through Florida.

They suggested that I go and ask for JJ Dillon and maybe I would get a chance to do a TV spot or two with them. So,

153

my brother Jimm and I went up early to the Huntington Civic Center, went to the back door and asked for JJ. We got in and we got on the card. Jimm wrestled a guy called, "The Black Bean Bandit."

This was when Piper was doing an angle with Ric Flair when Flair was doing the real world champ deal shortly after leaving WCW and taking the thirty pounds of gold with him. He and Piper were doing chair matches at the time.

While I was sitting on a table waiting to see who I would be working with that night, "The Rowdy One" sees me. At the time I was young, in decent shape, and had bleached blond hair.

"Hey kid! Who ya workin' tonight?" Of course I didn't have a clue who I was with yet as the board wasn't up. Anyway Piper comes over and officially introduces himself. Um, like I don't know who he is. But, he was just being a professional and doing the proper thing with an introduction and a handshake. He says come on over here for a minute. I follow him and we talk for a few minutes and he says, "Ya know, you look a little like Flair with that beached hair. I have an idea for ya if you're up to it."

We then walk into a bathroom that is in the back of the arena and he asked me to stay there and try not to be seen for a couple of minutes. "I'll be right back." I have no idea what he has planned, but, I stand there, in a bathroom in the backstage area of The Huntington Civic Center.

Yep, just standing there, wondering if this is some kind of a rib or what. After a couple of minutes pass, the door opens and not only is it Piper; he has Ric Flair with him. He introduces us to each other and runs his idea by Flair and myself. He thought that since I had the hair like Flair, that maybe he could come to the ring and pick up a chair, and say, "This chairs for Flair" before he gets in the ring, and then possibly use it on me as the match reaches its finish. Of course I agree to do it.

I go to the ring as, "Bobby Smedley from Ashland, Kentucky" and wait, and that's when I hear Piper's music. Bagpipes! I spit on him. I seriously spit right in his face. Anyway, he grabs a chair, and says, "This kid thinks he's Ric Flair. Well, I've got a chair for you Flair!"

As I said, I spit on him. This of course infuriates him more and gives him a reason to pick up the chair and threaten me with it. Hey, it was his idea; I never wanted to spit on Roddy Piper. Anyway, we have the match, which I called in the ring, a couple of quick turnbuckles, a backdrop, and a bull dog to finish, and "one, two, three," and I'm looking at the lights right before he goes and retrieves the chair. I'm getting up as he swings it at my head just as I'm making my way to and jumping over the top rope to escape. Perfect! Like he said in *They Live*, "I came here to chew bubble gum and kick ass. And I'm all out of bubble gum." He must have been out of bubble gum on this day, because he kicked my ass. I put him over then, and I would again. For the record, he was super light and easy to work with in the ring.

We spoke several times years later when he came into WCW. He was always a gentleman and a professional around me. He was in Vancouver when I was there for EA Sports. He was in town doing an episode of the television show *Viper* and was staying in the same hotel that we all were staying in. He spotted us at breakfast one morning before we had to go out for our motion capture shoot and came by and said hello as he was leaving and that he would be back later in the evening. "We'll have a couple of drinks boys" he said as he left with his driver. He didn't make it back until later that evening but he did leave us a couple rounds of drinks on a tab for us at the hotel bar. He never forgot what it was like being, "one of the boys." Thanks Hot Rod!

### ⊰ A Few More ⊱

I only met Paul Bearer a couple of times backstage when he was brought in with The Undertaker during a couple of weekend runs while in SMW. He was very professional. I always thought he was a great talker with his gimmick and of course, paired with Undertaker it was a great gimmick.

Al "The Master Blaster" Green was another guy who I met when I was still living in Florida. I'd see him around at the gym sometimes, or at a show or two, but it wasn't until years later while we both were in WCW that I was around him enough to get the know him a little better. Years later, a couple of guys I knew were traveling on business when they ran into him. Once he found out they were from Ashland and that they knew me, he told them to, "say hello to Bobby for me." It's always nice to be remembered.

Mark Starr was another Malenko guy who I really liked a lot. He had been at the school a couple of years before I made my way down to Florida. I first ran into him one day at a tanning salon. I was delivering pizzas and still training at the time. He was very pleasant and encouraging to me when I introduced myself to him. I was also working small shows then too, and would run into him here and there. He always encouraged me to keep training and always seemed to be a positive person to me when we spoke about wrestling. Once I got to WCW, I began to see him all the time. We got to work together on one of the World Wide TV tapings in Orlando. We had a really good solid old school match. I remember him chuckling a little bit when Terry Taylor asked him to put me over. Of course he had no problem doing so, but we both kind of laughed about it before the match. That's just the way this business is. Anyway, I always thought Mark was a real talent to be in the ring with, and I always enjoyed being around him.

"Gigolo" Jimmy Del Ray was another Florida guy who is no longer with us. I first met Jimmy while I was in Florida when he was wrestling under the name Jimmy Backlund. I saw him wrestling at the old Eddie Graham Sports Complex on a Sunday evening and struck up a conversation with him. I talked to him about training on some weekends down in Tampa at the Malenko Camp.

He only encouraged me saying Larry was a good trainer and to stick with it. I didn't see him for a while until I eventually moved down to Tampa and would see him wrestling at The Sportatorium. I always thought Jimmy was a very talented wrestler. I think his amateur background helped in how agile and athletic he was in the ring. Years later I was in the back of Freedom Hall in Johnson City, Tennessee prior to an SMW show and who walks in, none other than Jimmy. He told me he was going to be coming into SMW soon and of course, he did. Aong with Dr. Tom Prichard he became one half of the tag-team known as "The Heavenly Bodies," managed by James E. Cornette. He went on to work for several other companies including the WWF. If you knew Jimmy, he loved ribs and would even laugh at himself. It was funny to see him do his little taunting dance prior to or during a match and his stomach would jiggle. That's how he got stuck with the "gigolo" nickname.

As you know by now, after making contact with The Malenko Wrestling Academy I left Kentucky for Florida in order to pursue my dream of becoming a full-time professional wrestler. I first moved to Orlando and commuted to Tampa every weekend to train. There was a really wonderful lady who assisted The Great Malenko. That lady was Phyllis Lee. She used to make phone calls, give rides, run errands, and petty much did everything one can think of to help run a wrestling school and help young guys trying to get their careers off the ground.

Eventually a room opened up at her apartment so I ended up moving in with Ms. Lee. Sean Waltman, Willie Wilkerson Jr, and few others all came in and out, as did many other young guys. Some stayed weekends crashing on the couch after shows and others would just drop by to watch wrestling tapes, go to training together or catch a ride to shows. She was always supportive. She helped many of the boys through the years. Phyllis was a good woman with a heart of gold. We had a small falling out over something that was purely business, not personal, so towards the end of her life we weren't as close as we had once been. I did try to reach out to her more than once through mutual friends letting her know that I was always appreciative of her and thankful for her help early in my career. RIP Phyllis, you're missed by many, but not forgotten.

## ✎ Dusty Rhodes ✎

*The American Dream*

*"I have wined and dined with kings and queens
and I've slept in alleys and dined on pork and beans."*

One of the most charismatic and over guys in professional wrestling of all time was, "Star Dust" himself, "The American Dream" Dusty Rhodes. ICON! Dusty is one who is just that, an icon. In a world where we throw words like superstar, legend, and icon around way too much, that is not the case when it comes to Dusty. He was and is an Icon.

I only use that word to describe him and Piper, as they, in my humble opinion are the only two here, who were and are worthy to be considered true icons of the wrestling business. Dusty was an American Dream personified and a hero to his millions and millions of fans around the world.

His promos were some of the best of all time. He did pretty well for himself to be, "The son of a plumber." Watch his "Hard Times" promo. In part, "You don't know what hard times are daddy. Hard times are when the textile workers around this country are out of work, they got four or five kids and can't pay their wages, can't buy their food. Hard times are when the auto workers are out of work and they tell 'em to go home. And hard times are when a man has worked at a job for thirty years, thirty years, and they give him a watch, kick him in the butt and say 'hey a computer took your place, daddy,' that's hard times! That's hard times! And Ric Flair you put hard times on this country by takin' Dusty Rhodes out, that's hard times. And we all had hard times together, and I admit, I don't look like the athlete of the day supposed to look. My belly's just a lil' big, my heiny's a lil' big, but brother, I am bad. And they know I'm bad." Whether you're one of the boys, wanting to learn to do a promo, a fan who loves old school wrestling, or just someone who enjoys hearing someone speaking the truth and telling it like it is to make you believe. That is how you draw people into your angle and get people to believe in you. That's called "charisma."

There's so much I could say about Dusty, but so many already know what a great NWA Champion he was. Everyone already knows that he, "Wined and dined with kings and queens" and "slept in alleys and dined on pork and beans." Everyone knows he represented the common man. Everyone knows what a great booker he was and what a great mind he had for professional wrestling. Hell, he even had a finish named after him, "The Dusty Finish."

With all that said, all I can say is, it was an honor to have met Dusty Rhodes in person. It was one of the highlights of my career to hear his voice along with Tony Schiavone calling many of my matches on WTBS, "The mother ship if you will," on *WCW Saturday Night*. Thank you Dusty Rhodes for all you did and for all you gave to the world of professional wrestling. RIP Dream!

## ✦ Twelve ✦

*"Here is the test to find whether your mission on Earth is finished: If you're alive, it isn't."—Richard Bach*

## ✦ Concussions and Drain Bamage ✦

*"Repetitive head trauma chokes the brain! And turns man into something else."—Dr. Bennet Omalu, Concussion*

According to The Concussion Legacy Foundation: "A concussion is a serious injury to the brain resulting from the rapid acceleration or deceleration of brain tissue within the skull. Rapid movement causes brain tissue to change shape, which can stretch and damage brain cells. This damage also causes chemical and metabolic changes within the brain cells, making it more difficult for cells to function and communicate." http://concussionfoundation.org/ Please visit their website for further information. This isn't meant to be a term paper or some in-depth essay that I'm trying to get an A on in a college course. This is just my story and how concussions have affected my life. If nothing else, it will probably prove how little I actually know about concussions, so my best advice to you is, do your own homework if you or a loved one has suffered even one concussion. Having experienced many concussions myself, I know that they do affect your life and the way you think and behave, both short and long term.

When I started writing this book and specifically this chapter my youngest son had a concussion. He had hit his head while snowboarding. What had me so nervous about this concussion was it came only about three weeks after him having suffered one at a high school wrestling match just a couple of weeks prior. It was his second concussion within a three week span. He was wrestling a couple of weight classes up from his normal class against an older boy. His opponent had a little less experience and wasn't very coordinated. Anyway, after a quick take down, the boy lost his balance and fell on my sons head with his full body weight. It was a simple mistake and kind of a freak accident when he was trying to escape from being pinned. He got to his base, didn't actually escape, but then as both boys tumbled outside the ring on the mat, the boy just fell on my sons head. It wasn't intentional and after a brief time out they continued their match. Again, it wasn't intentional and was an accident. For the remainder of the day my son wasn't right. I should have known and did suspect that he had suffered a concussion, but he passed the sports medicine doctors quick exam and continued on with his matches. He was a little tired and somewhat dazed and confused but as I said, he did continue to wrestle throughout the tournament. After the weekend, we went to the doctor. He had suffered a concussion. He ended up taking some time off and everything appeared to be alright after a couple of days.

Fast forward about three weeks and that's when he hit his head while snowboarding. I took him to the emergency room where they did a CAT scan and x-rays of his neck and upper back area where he hit when he landed before a quick whip lash movement snapped his head back into the hard packed snow. Everything came back negative, but he was diagnosed with a concussion, again. Now, three weeks later he still hasn't been released from the hospital doctors care to participate in practice or meets. We went back to the "Impact Center" where they performed a battery of test and he didn't fare too well. He was still having throbbing headaches and still hadn't returned to school. He ended up missing the remainder of his wrestling season. I also had to enroll him in home school for almost three months due the severity of his concussion. On a positive note he eventually returned to school and finished out the school year. Every year, there are over 250,000 kids who are seen in emergency rooms across the United States with head injuries related to sports played at school and other recreational sports. That's a lot of head injuries.

Now, why is this so important to me, and why include this story in this book? Well, I've had thirteen documented concussions and I know how my brain is, and it's not right. Laugh, but it's true. The thirteen I mention are the ones that are accounted for, as I said, documented. How many other concussions do you think I've had through the years? I couldn't begin to tell you, but I know I've had more trauma to my head than most from playing organized sports since I was ten years old, plus the many years of playing basketball and football just for the exercise, fun, and for recreation. Who knows what kind of damage my head has sustained? I think many of my problems, personal and otherwise, stem from the injuries I've suffered from head trauma. I know a thing or two about concussions. Then again, I don't know anything about them. We as a society are just now beginning to research more about concussions and trying to get a better understanding about head injuries. We are just now hearing about how these head injuries, and especially head injuries where a concussion has occurred are possibly having long–term effects on our lives. How many concussions did I really have? I have no idea! I have suffered many head injuries. That is one thing I am sure of. I have stayed in games while playing sports because I, we, they (coaches) just didn't know any better than to let me keep playing. How many times had I been hit in the head playing street football? I do recall two times where once myself and a big strong kid from Cleveland hit heads so hard on a tackle we both must have laid on the ground for ten or fifteen minutes before even moving. I recall another time playing some tackle football right before getting into wrestling. As I tackled this guy, who was as big as an NFL linebacker, we hit head-on with each other. We both tried to laugh it off as we sat there on the ground. Everyone was taking a break talking about how hard a hit it was by both of us. There have just been too many times when I've suffered head trauma that I seriously believe affected my long term health, and especially my mental health.

Let me repeat the number of documented concussions I've suffered, it's thirteen. Yes, you read that right, thirteen. The first concussion I ever got was when I was nine years old. My last one happened a couple years back when my brother and I were in a car wreck in which a lady ran a stop sign and t-boned our car on the passenger side, which is where I was seated. Of the thirteen, nine of them, all of which have been documented, came from professional wrestling matches. I know many professional wrestlers who have worked right through matches and continued working the next few days without even being checked. I know I have. A couple of concussions I recall from my days in the ring do stand out in my memory for some reason. I received one when I was thrown through a bathroom door in a high school gym while working for SMW. I had no idea a solid brick retaining wall was on the other side of that door.

I was out on my feet and don't recall anything after that point. I continued working the rest of the loop and to this day I don't remember what towns I was in or how I even got home. I also suffered one in WCW taking a sunset flip off the middle rope. I didn't feel I was that high off the ground, but I do remember hitting the back of my heard extremely hard upon impact in the ring. Again, I'm not sure how I finished the match. I do know I was put on a red-eye flight back home from California. Again, I'm not complaining, just stating the facts.

Think about having a constant headache for 24 hours or for a few days on end. You go through the motions or moments and a few days pass before you realize that the hours have actually turned into days. That's not a good sign nor is it a good feeling when trying to function in everyday society. I'm not complaining and I certainly have no regrets because I am the one who chose this life when I first entered the world of pro wrestling. I'm just saying that people need to take better care of their health in regards to head injuries and concussions. A lot of people don't realize how severe a concussion is when someone suffers one. It's a head trauma, your brain has been shifted, even the severity of whiplash can cause a concussion, and it's not just getting a ding to the head or landing on it night after night. I know one of my doctors told me that even taking a turnbuckle night after night after your opponent shoots you into one is equivalent to being in a car wreck every night and someone rear ends you at twenty miles per hour. It's internal, so some people just don't think you're really hurt, or may not believe that you have personal issues brought on by a concussion or in my case, at least thirteen of them. I think many of my problems are concussion related. Concussions again, think about having a constant headache 24 hours a day for several days on end. You go through the motions or moments and days pass before you realize that hours have turned into days, that can't be good, hell, it's not good. I know! Post-concussion syndrome, it's like maybe mine, or the

163

combination of concussions haven't ever gone away. I don't like to be in the real world, that's why I stay in and to myself many times. I know it's hard or damn near impossible to work a normal job. There are just too many memory problems, hard to focus on the task at hand, and concentration problems. I have headaches, some more severe than others, and I do deal with those pretty well. But, I think my aggressive, argumentative behavior is a direct result of concussions.

I think that I probably have what's known as Second Impact Syndrome, or SIS. Some die from that second or third impact when the head injuries occur. Others, the survivors like me, suffer from lifelong problems and disabilities. If you've had a concussion, or as many as I have, here are a few truths I do know from personal experience. One, you're prone to violent outburst, two, there's many times when you deal with depression, and three, those depressing thoughts tend to lead to suicidal thoughts. For the most part, I try to stay positive. I deal with my depression in different ways, but again, I usually kick out of any funk or mood of feeling depressed after a couple of days when I feel like I'm getting a little bit down. I usually try not to think bad thoughts. If I find myself getting to a bad place or feel off a bit or too far gone, I tell myself over and over, just keep going on, and just keep getting up every day. You have reasons to live and you have the gift of life. My time here is not done yet. I have to tell myself this over and over. I know I have more to give in this life. I do realize suicide isn't the final solution.

We all are just now reading about and learning more about how concussions have affected some of these former NFL football players. The movie, *Concussion* was recently released as of this writing. There are other athletes who have suffered multiple head injuries during their careers as well. It's so important to understand or try to understand what some of these studies are finding out about what kind of brain damage we may have actually suffered, or long-term damage acquired after having a concussion or multiple head injuries or head trauma.

Dr. Bennet Omalu found dark tangles of tau protein that he believed had choked the brain from the inside out. It was

164

Omalu's autopsy of Mike Webster and those he performed on a couple of other former NFL players who had committed suicide that really started making headlines and bringing CTE to the attention of the public. Chronic Traumatic Encephalopathy, or CTE, kept turning up in the brains of several other former players who also suffered from mental illness and they eventually committed suicide. That's basically the short of it; you can watch the film and see. You will recognize the name of each of the players involved.

Sadly, more and more guys who played in the NFL or are involved in high impact sports and combat sports like boxing, MMA, and wrestling will eventually suffer a concussion or maybe even a few during their career. Again, this is just my take on what I have experienced and again, I'm not trying to write a text book on concussions. You make up your own mind and educate yourself about concussions. I would highly recommend that if you are in a sport or have an accident that causes you to have a concussion, don't take it lightly. Make sure you get checked out, and take time off. Your health and maybe your life may be at risk if you continue to keep having head injuries or concussion symptoms. Parents, please watch your children who play in youth sports and especially the ones who are involved in contact or combat sports. Lastly, don't take my word for it when it comes to concussions, educate yourself.

## ◆ Aging Gracefully ◆

As I move along towards finishing this second book, I'm becoming less nervous about it and more and more excited. I hit a wall just a little bit before sitting my ass down and typing all the notes and stories I had written over the last couple of years. I had this conclusion about, "Taking it home" written down and finished before I actually had the stories completed. The biggest obstacle besides sitting and typing was realizing and accepting my real age. I went through a little two week period where I was really struggling with getting older. Maybe it was bit like a little mid-life crisis, I really don't know. Of course getting older at least beats the alternative as I'm still alive. It's like George Burns once said, "You can't help getting older, but you don't have to get old."

What I do know was that I needed to kick out of it and kick out fast as I'm not getting any younger, and that was exactly what the little mental breakdown was all about anyway.

I'm fifty-two years old, hell, I'll be fifty-three by the time this book is published, but, damn fifty-two was hard on me. It was a year I had some type of serious revelation that I wasn't fifty anymore and probably couldn't get by trying to say I'm fifty even though I been saying I was fifty since I was forty-eight. They say age is just a number, but for whatever reason that number hit me hard on a personal level this year. I was getting my hair cut a few months back as I usually only have two cuts per year, one in June around my birthday and six months later around Christmas time, exactly six months apart. Well, when I got this last haircut I saw a lot of hair on the floor and just looked at it and knew, "That's the last time I'll see any blond or natural color in my hair." Then as I looked into the mirror, I saw just how much gray I had in my hair. Whoa! Gray was here and it was here to stay. A few months passed and that's when a couple of younger girls I talk to told me what I already knew. "Bobby, that's a lot of gray, it's got more gray than blond..." and then the more merciful, "But it looks good, it's not that bad...it looks alright..." But I know I'm not that young anymore, and any adoration from girls that age will become just a little bit more of a challenge for me to get than it used to be. But I realize I'm getting older and I'm fine with that so long as I do so gracefully.

I'd like to think I have aged pretty gracefully so far. I also think, that as much damage as I have done to my body through the years of wrestling, by being active when I was younger, and because of wresting, I did put off a few of life's tougher ages to face. What's age anyway? Some say it's nothing more than a number, but some numbers can be more harsh than others. Other than a few gray hairs here's how I hit some of those numbers.

They say once you hit thirty, your metabolism slows down and weight gain comes easy and fast, and it's harder to take it off once you gain it. Not so much with me. Well, when I hit thirty I was wrestling full time and actually had a really good match that night in some small Kentucky town for SMW against a guy who was nine years my junior.

I didn't have that little bit of extra weight that everyone talked about being so hard to take off. It wasn't until about three months after I turned thirty-two that I started gaining weight and found it a little harder to take off or to keep it off over the next couple of years. So I offset thirty by two years, plus I still had a full head of hair, all blond with a trace of red.

When forty rolled around I was still wrestling. Sure by now I had gained some weight, but still no gray hairs. Yeah, age was catching up to me as my body was breaking down, which it eventually did. As I told someone on a podcast recently, "My body is more fucked up than a can of fishing worms." It wasn't until I turned forty-three that I started to see a couple of gray hairs. Again, score one for me as The Big Four O didn't bother me too much because I didn't see the gray and still had a full head of hair. I have several lingering injuries that I deal with daily. Due to the injuries I've had, well they'll be with me the rest of my life. It's physically impossible for me to even entertain the thought of, "having that one more match." For me, it has to be 100% or nothing. I have a diminishing musculature and arthritic joints. I have bone on bone in my right knee. I have trouble hearing out of my right ear. "Say what one more time!" And, as mentioned earlier, I'm quite sure many of my problems are CTE related. All of this affects my overall health, but I'm not going to bitch and complain because no matter how fucked up my body may be, I still feel like I am aging gracefully. So, here comes fifty. Bada boom bada bang! Fifty came and went and I only had a small amount of gray. It wasn't until I hit the half way mark through my fifty second year that I, well, as you're reading the story, I have more gray in my hair than not. It's when I finally realized, "Damn, you're not that young anymore." But hey, I still have a full head of hair and who cares if it has some, well more than some gray to it? I'm just lucky to be alive let alone worry about my hair. Obviously my hair has always been important to me. People have always complimented me on it since I was in my youth. I attribute this to one time having it blessed by a little old lady who had a full head of thick hair when I was young. So, I guess that's why I kind of went through this little crisis.

Anyway, I kicked out on two, because that's what I do. Plus, I realize, "Life moves pretty fast. If you don't stop and look around once in a while, you could miss it" as Ferris Bueller said, so I'm trying not to have bad days worrying over my hair. I'm just trying to age gracefully. I'd like to think I am as I was recently told by a man I have a lot of love and respect for, Dr. Bob Reynolds, PhD, "Smed, you remind me of cross between a young Kris Krisofferson and Hemingway." I'll take that compliment any day of the week. Those words right there meant more to me about how I was aging than anything I had ever heard or thought. Hey, Krisofferson was a good looking, handsome man, and a Rhodes Scholar. Ernest Hemingway, need I say more? So yeah, I'm aging gracefully.

*If I was a Kris Krisofferson or a Hemingway*
*Oh what I a man I would be*
*I would be a man*
*But, I would still only be me.*

## ⚜ A Love Letter Revisited ⚜

*"I hate myself for loving you*
*Can't break free from the things that you do*
*I wanna walk but I run back to you*
*That's why I hate myself for loving you"*
*Joan Jett*

I used to love you, hell, maybe I still do. I never minded when you walked away from me; maybe I'm the one who walked away. You didn't pull me back in. I crawled back to you just like you had waltzed right back into my life.

Maybe I called you a slut or even a cheap whore, but I'm the one who whored myself out for you. I never minded as I gladly paid you, and I paid you often and paid you well. I'm still paying! But, I'm glad I got my chance to see you, meet you, and be with you, and even fall in love with you.

The passion I felt when you first kissed me, even when you bit me, it was beyond any feeling that I had ever experienced on any level in my life before nor have I since. Broken down and with a heavy heart, shivers run down my spine, I offer forgiveness as I open my arms up to you willingly because you're the one constant which actually brought me happiness.

The young, innocent and naive boy is no more. Older, without innocence, and oh so much wiser, looking back at all those years. The pains were and are worth it. Like a scar, every one of those memories tells a story...the story of me...the story of you...the story of us.

My mind, my heart, they forgive you just as I begin to understand this familiar relationship. My body, well, it has a hard time with forgiveness. As it gets older, and as the aches and pains become more noticeable, it is stubborn and is not so quick to forgive, but it does. Those aches and pains all have a story to tell. Many men will never understand this unconditional love for you, but I do, as does my body.

Those sleepless nights are just a reminder of the years I spent on the road traveling to the next town or just to get back home. The annoyance in my left shoulder when I try to turn over at night is a constant reminder of being locked in an arm bar, or perhaps from a beautifully executed arm drag. It's real!

My neck, so sore, tender, and tight, oh how you keep me up. I lay thinking about the days when I could bridge, days when I had a strong neck, and could lift others over my body while pinning them flat on their back. My mind drifts back to when I was one of the few who could actually do a Northern Lights Suplex, but then it quickly shifts gears to when I was one of the first to ever take a power bomb off the top rope. Performing those moves only solidifies my love for you and the passion I had to please my fans and your fans from around the world in your name. Is there any wonder why I'm so tight every day and night?

My back is so stiff that it's hard to sit or to stand for any extended length of time, and that's another reminder of my love for you. I of course do sit, stand, and even walk as I'm one of the lucky ones. At times it's through sheer will, as I can do so while thinking about taking the perfect bump for you. The stiffness is a reminder of many rings that we've shared as I lie there in my bed, still dreaming of only you.

Good morning sunshine is what I'd like to hear, but the grinding noise from my knees, is what I hear. The bone on bone friction is also what I feel. But, there's no complaining as not only am I six feet over instead of six foot under, I can live another day and the pains in my knees are mere reminders of the thousands of knee drops and Hindu squats I once performed through the years as a fine tuned athlete. There's no shame in my love for you.

My heart still pumps excitedly whenever I'm around you. That adrenaline still accelerates whenever I get the chance to visit you. I suck it up and endure these pains to be around you my seductive mistress. I still love my princess through it all...

I'm still that kid who wants to believe. I'm that fan who tries to believe. I'm one of the boys who tries to make others believe. I'm still your man and you're still my favorite girl. Pro Wrestling, my lust, my desire, my love, my mistress, no matter how bad my body hurts and my heart breaks, I still love you. I love you! PRO WRESTLING!

## ❧ Thirteen ❧

*"I don't care if the average guy on the street really knows
what I'm like, as long as he knows I'm not really a mean,
vicious guy. My friends and family know what I'm really like.
That's what's important."—Don Rickles*

## ❧ John David Johnson ❧

S.E. Hinton said, "If you have two friends in your
lifetime, you're lucky. If you have one good friend, you're
more than lucky." My question is, "How lucky am I?"
Through my good friend, Danny Phillips, I met a guy by the
name of Dave Johnson, more specifically, John David
Johnson. He became a good friend of mine from an early age
on. Dave had a heart of gold, fist of iron and a big silver
tooth. That's right, other than his height and muscular size;
one of the first things one would notice was his big silver
tooth. Many, to this day still remember him having that silver
tooth if they remember nothing else. But, I dare say, if
anyone ever met Dave, they will remember more than that
about him.

If you can count your true friends on one hand during
the course of your life, you're damn lucky. I'm not talking
about acquaintances; I'm talking about true friends. He was
the kind of person who, if your life depended on it, they
would be there by your side. Are you able to count your true
friends on one hand? More often than not, the list of friends
that you can count on one hand changes throughout the
course of your life. Times change, circumstances change,
and life just happens. It happens, friends come and go in and
out of your life all the time, but I'll bet no matter what, you
will always remember those select few who you can call a
true friend.

Dave was a tried and true friend. He was a loyal friend.
Of the many things he was, he was a loyal friend, not just to
me, but to anyone who was his friend or ran around with
him. With all of his friends and all of the friendships that he
had formed, the one constant was his loyalty. Loyalty in
friendship, that's something that seems to be rare these

days in our fast paced society. Dave had the kind of loyalty that you take to your grave.

There's a line in the movie *Platoon* that always reminds me of Dave. Its right after Elias has been killed and the guys are all down in the bunker hanging out, partying a little, talking and feeling sorry about themselves and what has happened, when Rhah says, "Elias didn't ask you to fight his battles for him. And if there's a heaven, and, God, I hope there is, I know he's sitting up there drunk as a fucking monkey and smoking shit, 'cause he done left his pains down here."

Everyone can have their own thoughts and beliefs when it comes to death. I'm not here to pass my beliefs on to you. Maybe this is really all there is. No Hell...No Heaven... Life is here. The reward is here, Pain is here. But, if there really is a heaven, I'm sure Dave is there. He done went on and left his pain down here over twenty years ago.

### ❧ My Brother ❧

*From Jimmy Mac to Sir James to Kenny Wynn and a Few Things in Between*

I've made mention of my brother Jimm before, but I probably haven't said enough good things about the guy. I used to refer to him as my older brother by four years because I was so much better looking than him, plus, well, I looked younger. Hey, I said this book is true, so believe what you will. My brother's full name is James Atley Smedley. He went from being called Jimmy to Jimmy Mac, back to just Jimmy. Then he was called, "Little Smed" then "Smed." Eventually he changed the spelling of his name from Jim to Jimm. He also had a few names in pro wrestling along the way and somewhere in between went back to Jimm. Either way, either name, he's my brother and I'm very proud of the man he has become.

He is there for me through thick and thin and I think he knows how much I love him, but just in case he doesn't, I'm putting it out there now. He's a Chaplain for Hospice and also works in several local hospitals as a bereavement counselor as well. Yes, I'm aware that it's been mentioned in the book before but this is for him and I have to write it the way I tell

172

it, in my own words. It takes a special kind of person to perform the kind of work he does and for that, a man like him deserves a lot of love and a ton of respect, not just from me, but from the families and people he serves. I hear from people all the time what a wonderful job he did at so and so's funeral, or that he came to visit them when they were in the hospital or did them a seemingly small favor that actually was something big for them in their time of need. That's Special! But, I'm going to share a couple of other stories that always stand out in my mind about Jimm.

He'll always be, "Lil Ol' Jim Mac" to me in many regards as I've seen him grow up. For you youngsters out there, there was a song way back in 1966 called *Jimmy Mack* by Martha and the Vandellas. I also had a couple of aunts who were in their late teens to early twenties, and when Jimmy was born, they used to sing him that song all the time. At least that's the way I always remembered it. Okay, I'm four years older than him, so yes, I watched him grow up. What many people don't know about him is how tough a kid he

*My brother Jimm,*
*one of the good guys.*

was while we were growing up. I've seen him head butt an older kid, in a head butting contest, and the other guys tooth chipped and fell out. He head butted him in the forehead and the guys tooth fell out, yes you read that right. Now, what starts such a thing, or why does someone have a head butting contest? I'll explain: It's because when we were in grade school, when this happened I, along with several friends, saw him tackle a Cadillac and leave a dent in the bumper. Now, I'm not kidding. We were playing football and he caught a pass and ran smack dab right into a parked Cadillac. This was in the seventies mind you, back when cars had the big old chrome bumpers, unlike these lil sissy fiber glass bumpers on cars today. It was thick, shiny and chrome! Except now it had a dent in it from my brothers' head. Talk about hard headed. Well, I go to school and tell a couple of guys and some believe me as they had younger brothers who had played football with him and knew him, and I'm sure more than a few were skeptical.

One of them bravely said that his little brother's head was harder than my little brothers' head, and well, that's how one ends up in a head butting contest. It took place several days later at the morning bus stop and the two boys exchanged a couple of head butts until the one boy's tooth chipped and fell out. Guess who won that contest? Yep, Jim Mac! My Brother!

Another time we were slap boxing on our knees in our bed and we had an open window behind us. Well, lucky for Jimm we were on the first floor at the time because he took a back bump right out the window. I panicked thinking not only could he be dead, but our mom was in the living room just outside of our door and if she heard the commotion she'd be madder than hell. I quickly looked over the edge of the window and there about four feet down was Jimm looking up laughing. I'm not sure how he landed or how he didn't get hurt but he wasn't, so I quickly grabbed his outstretched arm and he Batman walked back up the side of the house and into the window right about the time the door swung open as mom asked us, "What's going on in here?" With the smile of two innocent angels in unison, we both said, "nothing." I told you he was tough.

Again, these are just little stories from our childhood that make me smile or laugh out loud sometimes when I think about some of the reasons that make me love him so much. I also personally introduced him to, "The Clothes Line." He had this little Snoopy dog that had wheels on it that he would ride around the house. Outside our house we had a long sloping driveway that led to a garage. One day I get this bright idea to encourage my little dare devil of a brother to ride his Snoopy Mobile down to the bottom. Little did he know, I had tied some fishing line across the middle of the slope and when he came down, I pulled, and well, clothes line city sucker, gotcha. Man, that wasn't meant to sound mean and I truly had no intention of hurting him, but he took a good bump, had a good sized red mark across his neck and a huge bump and cut on the back of his head. Yeah, sorry about that Jimm, I didn't think that one all the way through, but hey, it made you tough and we can laugh about it now. Can't we? You know a little practice what you preach kind of thing, forgiveness? See, I told you he was not only tough, but a good man as well.

Jimm was always a good athlete and I always thought that he would have made a really good professional wrestler. He actually did train and even had more matches than many people know about, nor would he probably want me telling everyone about. But he did! And, I'm going to share just a couple with you. He wrestled on more than one fund raiser as, "Sir James." He did a, "Spicy Hot" gimmick and a couple of others along the way as well. My personal favorite was when he worked as, "Kenny Wynn." He went to train some with me over at Malenko's a few times when we shared an apartment together back in the day. He trained on the weights every day with me at one time, and he trained in the ring with me and many others through the years. I personally always thought he would have or could have been better than I ever was and that's a shoot. We always had fun working matches together because that was time well spent.

It was an added bonus if I got to work with him because I always knew I'd have a good match, a fun match, and it would be an entertaining match. He was that good. He knew how to work and knew ring psychology. That always makes it easier when you can work with someone who knows what the hell they're doing in the ring, and he did.

Oh, by the way, sorry about that time when I tombstoned you in the ring and right as you went to inhale, the sweat from my belly dripped right into your mouth. I guess that kind of makes up for my chipped teeth from your pile driver, so can we call that one even? Anyway, James Atley Smedley, you're a good man. You chose a much higher calling than professional wrestling and that was a life of serving God and your fellow man, and for that, I only have Love and Respect for you. Yep, Jimm Smedley is a pretty good little brother to have and I'm damn proud of him. Thanks Jimm.

# ✒ My Family ✒

If you read my first book, you know my dad left my mother, my brother and myself when I was quite young. Sometimes the things that seem so negative at the times end up becoming something more positive in one's life. This is kind of what happened to me. My mom, bless her heart, eventually did remarry. She didn't marry Mr. Right, but she did marry Mr. Romans. Romans was kind of a Clint Eastwood looking guy who was probably born a few years too late. He wore jeans, pointed toe cowboy boots, and shirts that resembled those worn in the old Wild West. He was a good man. My brother and I only knew him as Romans. That was his last name, and back then that's what many thought his first and only name was. I guess they dated for a couple of years. Being young, I really didn't know they were dating, I just knew he came around a lot and was nice to my brother and me. He had three children from a previous marriage, two sons and a daughter. He and my Mom married on September 1, 1973. It was within a year of Mom getting remarried that my brother and I called him Dad. To lil' ol' Jimmy Mac, that was really the only Dad he ever knew. Myself, I knew my Dad, and had been around him some, but for all intents and purposes, Romans was the only Dad I ever had as well. Now keep in mind this was the 1970's and believe it or not, Romans got custody of his children and we became a family of four boys, one girl, and a eventually another boy would arrive. So, in addition to myself and Jimm, there was now Danny, Wayne, Debi, and the baby, Steven. We weren't *The Brady Bunch* by any means, but we were a family. That's a lot of mouths to feed. Romans was probably the hardest working man I've ever met in my life. His job was that of hard labor. He could do anything with his hands, and he was always thinking up ideas to keep busy to make money. He worked in construction, and when that job was over, he would rush home to eat, only to head back out the door to some second job that he had set up on the side to provide extra income to support our family. Both my parents are now deceased having passed away within 18 months of one another. That was a tough time to go through, but, I was there for both of them through their dying days. I was lucky enough to help take care of them the best way I could, just like they had taken care of me all those years. Don't get me wrong, I'm no saint, and deserve no special reward. All I did was check on them every day, take them some meals, or get them out of the house if they felt up to it. I'd run them to the doctors, pick up their medications, and drop off groceries as needed. Many times, I would just visit by running by their house to check on them and have lunch with them.

Through the years, as many know, situations and times change. I have a best friend, Danny Phillips, and wrote some about him before. We've been best friends for over forty years. I was the little brother he never had, and he was the big brother I never had. It has worked out pretty well for us through the years. I practically lived with him and his family while growing up. His dad Dan Ed was a hard-working man who I always respected as a father figure. His mom Judy was a big influence on my life and could be viewed as my second mother. The Phillips family is my family.

Again, as circumstances change some people come into your life when you least expect it. Right around the time my parents got sick, an old friend of mine from high school came back into my life. Bobby Reynolds and I had known each other for years through sports, but didn't get to become good friends until we reached high school. We ran track together back then, and it was around that time that we both began lifting weights. His dad also helped coach our track team along with our regular coach. We really got close during those early days back in the weight room. Both of us drifted apart but right when I needed someone in my life as I was going through the difficulty of dealing with sick parents, his family stepped in and became my second family.

He needed someone in his life as much as I needed someone in my life. We both have explosive personalities and were dealing with a lot of anger issues. We kind of calmed each other when we would get together to talk about the things we were dealing with during the last few years. He and his sister Jessie are just like my real brother and sister. I love them and their families like my own. His dad, Bob, or "Dr. Bob," is a man who holds a PhD and is probably the smartest man I've ever known. He's a thinker and he has had an interest in my life all the way back to, as I mentioned, my track days and early lifting days. He was the first person who ever told me, "Hey Smed. Don't sweat the small stuff, And it's all small stuff." I've never forgotten that. I can remember exactly where I was standing when he told me that. He's just a good man and his wife, Betty is just as good a person as one could ever meet. I sincerely think the Reynolds family saved me from myself at a time when I needed love most in my life. They loved and accepted me unconditionally. I've often said true family isn't always related by blood but by love, well the Reynolds's are my family by love.

Now that you've met the Romans, Phillips and the Reynolds families, meet the Smedleys. Of course there's me, and I have two sons, Drake and Brady. Drake has a year left in the Marine Reserves and is a diesel mechanic. He and his wife Hollie recently added another Smedley to the clan. I now have my new and precious little granddaughter, Lucy. Lucy loves her "Pops." "Baby Lucy," wow, she is such a blessing in my life. Talk about something life changing, when you have that first grandchild, there's no other feeling like it in the world. Brady recently graduated and is taking a year off from school and working. He is saving his money and hopes to become a snow board instructor one day. He's an avid snowboarder and loves the outdoors. I wish him much success and happiness. I love having them all around and enjoy spending time with them whenever we can.

Jimm, who I already mentioned has three children, Atley, Shelby, and Bailee. He really is a special kind of person. I'm not surprised to hear from others about what an awesome job he does as a bereavement counselor. I always knew that he would do something great with his life. I'm proud of you Jimm! That's about it. I keep my circle of family and friends tight. I love each of them in a special way.

To all my family, "SO MUCH!" Y'all know, so much, as in so much LOVE in the world. And, all my love goes to all of you.

### ❧ Formal Education ❧

*They liked me so much in school they always kept me extra.*

While reading this little part about the education of a wrestler or at least about some of the lessons learned, this may not seem to be wrestling related, but believe me it is. See, where I went to grade school when I first moved here, here of course being Ashland, Kentucky, the grade school I went to was for grades one through six. Well they liked me so much, they kept me for eight years. I repeated the first grade and two years of summer school. See I told you they liked me. Actually it was to teach me to learn to read and write. In Baltimore, the only thing I remember learning was, "Try to stay in the lines when you color," and "Robert, stop looking at the boats out in the bay." I also remembered having a, *Chitty Chitty Bang Bang* lunch box, but I don't remember getting much of an education. I did like looking out the windows and day dreaming an awful lot. So, when I started or should I say restarted the first grade here shortly after 1969, the teacher had us sit in a circle for reading time. This was very new to me. "See Dick run. See Jane run" and "See Spot run" seemed to be coming off the lips and from the voices of the other boys and girls rather smoothly, but I never knew who Dick, Jane, and Spot were. I had no idea why we were watching them run.

So, when the pretty little girl next to me handed me the book to take my turn to read, I polity asked in all seriousness, "Where's the crayons?" That's all I had ever done at my old school, day dream and draw pictures of the sail boats out on the water. Either they weren't teaching me to read or I had art class for eight hours per day, because I never remembered, even to this day, ever learning to read while in the first grade in Baltimore. All the other kids laughed at the new kid who didn't know how to read and asked for a box of crayons. Houston, we have a problem. I'm not so sure how dumb a box of rocks is, but I've heard the expression, "He's about as dumb as a box of rocks" through the years, so I guess, that's about how smart I was or was made to feel, about as dumb as a box of rocks. Education, none. Lesson learned? Learn to read.

So, as I mentioned, they kept me around for another round of first grade after my first go at it and then sent me to summer school as an added bonus. Summer school actually was kind of cool. I got to ride a school bus, and that was at a time when they didn't have buses in the Ashland elementary school system. And, as another added bonus there were kids there as dumb as me, and we got to take longer recesses in between reading lessons.

On the plus side of things, a free lunch was provided. "Damn," pretty cool, they pick you up on a school bus, you get to play with other children on recess, feed you, and all I have to do is try to learn to read. Um, Okay.

Obviously, I write like I talk, and yes, even in grade school I used "curse words." My education was coming right along. Lesson learned? Riding the bus is fun, recess was exciting, and lunch was pretty good, well, because it was food, and at my house we didn't have much food. Oh yeah, remember this all took place right after my mom was suckered into moving from Baltimore, where we had family to Ashland by my real father, where we had basically no family at the time. Yep, you guessed it. He moved out shortly after the move. Prick!

My mom worked with me and taught me more about reading, as she was an avid reader and wanted desperately for me to learn to read. And with the help of those summer school teachers and teacher's aides, I learned how to read "See Spot run." But, I still had to go back for that second year of first grade, so I did. Hey, I told you they liked me so much they wanted to keep me there.

First grade the second time around wasn't as fun as summer school. The only thing I remember was that for half of the day I got to see some of the kids who had advanced to second grade as I got to do the music, art, and gym classes with them, but still had to do the academic stuff back with my normal, first grade second time around classmates. Education? I passed first grade. Lesson learned? "See Dick, Jane and Spot run." Now get ready for summer school again, we really like you here.

It was also around the time I entered the second grade for the first time that I had the pleasure of being pulled from the classroom setting once a week to go meet with a man by the name of Mr. White. Mr. White was a tall, kind of balding man who had excellent posture. He spoke in a kind and gentle voice as the words rolled off his tongue with elegance and with intelligence. Yes, when I said I had the pleasure of being pulled from class it was with sarcasm, as it was rather

180

embarrassing having to leave my class mates to go visit a speech therapist once a week with other kids from other classes. In reality, it was a blessing and I'm thankful that Mr. White took the time to work on me with my speech impediment. I used to say all my "th" sounds like an "f," as in "thought would be fought," and "three" would sound like "free," as in "one, two, free." My "sh" sounds had a serious lisp and saying any of those words just came out all, "thucked up." I kid. I never had a problem with my F-words.

Anyway, after getting through six grades in eight years, I finally got to go to junior high school. It was while I was at Coles Jr. High School, playing sports, and out in the streets, well, that is where my real education started. It was a cool place that saw me through some tough times, but, I met friends who are still friends to this day, and I actually started to learn some book lessons as well.

From there of course came high school where I did alright. But honestly, even after finishing two years of junior college, dropping out to get into wrestling, then re-entering college later to finish my degrees, I still can't spell. I have a hard time reading out loud if ever asked to, so I usually try to remember what I read so when I do read it out loud, I jump, miss, and skip words, even though I read two or three books a week in private. I love reading. I dare say, I'm an avid reader like my mom was, but it just takes me longer to read than most. Education, I can read and write. Lesson learned? Perseverance!

"April Fools' Day, that's the only day for a man my age to return to college." I remember writing that in my first journal upon finally returning to college/university to try to finish completing my college education in communications. I was 39 years old. See, when I dropped out of college at the ripe old age of 21, I already knew everything. All I wanted to do was lift weights and wrestle. I was on the twenty two year plan of finishing my degree. I just got a little side tracked along the way. With that said, I went on to receive my Bachelor of Science in Communication from Ohio University, and my Master of Arts in Leadership and Liberal Arts from Duquesne University. I'm extremely proud of my degrees. Hey! I DID IT! Perseverance!

You're reading this book because, just like in *Pin Me Pay Me, Have Boots Will Travel*, I didn't give up on writing it. I read every day. I write every day. I never gave up on writing and finishing my first book, and I won't stop or give up on finishing this one. I'm a big believer in perseverance. I kicked out on two. I got back up, and I kept on moving onwards and upwards! That's the education of a wrestler!

## ∽ Going to the Finish ∾

So as my life moves forward, I try to stay as positive as possible and often times that's a hard thing for me to do. I find myself living my life my way, and that's only because it's the only way I know. I still wake up in the mornings reflecting on some goofy dream I've usually had from the night before. It's normally something like me being at an indie wrestling show that has drawn a pretty big house, thus I know it's a dream. Anyway, not only am I at the show, I'm commonly scheduled to go out and wrestle later on the show. But I never quite make it to the ring.

Rarely do I dream about actually being in the ring itself. Something or someone always stops me from making it all way down to ringside and from climbing into the ring. Mike Mooneyham, pro wrestling columnist and member of The Pro Wrestling Hall of Fame summed it up best, "Time to go home. In pro wrestling jargon, the expression is used as a form of communication to signal that it's time to go to the finish of a match. A savvy veteran always knows when it's time to go home." When I have these vivid dreams, I clearly know that it's, "Time to go home." They are a good reflection of the fact that I'll never climb back into a ring for a match again. Just like in the ring, you know when it's time to go home. I know it's time to bring this book to an end.

Once again I appreciate that you bought it and took the time to read it. It's my hope that you enjoyed it. I hope you even learned something by reading it. I hope I took you to places in your mind that made you recall some of those special moments that professional wrestling has brought you in your life. Please feel free to leave me a review at amazon.com/author/bobbyblaze I sincerely appreciate all fair and honest reviews.

The one thing I'm not doing is ever feeling sorry for myself or crying in my beer. I wouldn't trade nor wish my life on anyone else, ever. I just feel very fortunate to be alive today. I'm alive! I would not change the life I've had and my life experiences with anyone else in the world. Why would I? I have no reason to. I was fortunate enough to actually live my dream. I'm very fortunate. I got to do things and see things that many others never had the opportunity to do in their lives. All I can say about that is, if you have a dream, make it a reality. As I mentioned before, author Richard Bach said, "Here is the test to find whether your mission on Earth is finished: if you're alive, it isn't." My mission is not complete. It's never too late to set new goals. Of course one must work hard to achieve those goals, and then give it your best shot. I did, and I will again. I know my mission here isn't complete because I have more books to write and more people to help. I have a whole lot of living to do and dreams to live.

Nowadays I still read a lot of books, watch a lot of movies, and watch some sports on television. Every once in a while I enjoy a cold beer. I do get out with my friends from time to time. Some of those friendships were formed over forty years ago. That's a good thing, having people in your life who have been lifelong friends.

My needs are being met and I try to enjoy my life. As I said, I live a pretty quiet life. I go by the local store or deli on a daily basis to do some shopping and to play my daily lottery. The people I play the lottery with each day are my friends. The other day Brady found some old lottery tickets in a closet. He comes into the room holding some lottery tickets up and says, "Dad, I found these in the closet from 1998. What numbers are on them?" "What year?" "98."

I looked up at him and said, "000, 473, 210, and 310." He popped big time. He said that he knew I would know what the numbers were. I have a great long-term memory but can't tell you what I did yesterday. I have a terrible short-term memory. I've always played 473 for some odd reason, and then I started playing triple zeros while working for SMW. Once Drake was born I added 210 and then when Brady came along I started playing 310 for the month and dates of their birthdays. When he said ninety-eight, I knew it had to be those four numbers. Not bad for a guy who has had 13 concussions.

I stay in touch with some of the guys who I used to wrestle or travel with, but those times are rare. In the wrestling business it's hard to have a lot of true friends. A lot of these guys I've known for over twenty years. But, in this business many have become just mere acquaintances. I'm fine with that as time waits for no man and we all move on. I do miss many of them and I do miss the business, but only in my mind. My body reminds me every day about the life and lifestyle that I once lived.

I'm at peace with living a pretty quiet life nowadays. I try to keep a positive mindset because I've battled depression and know how low one can fall if they don't keep a positive attitude. I like trying to give back and helping others when I can. That always makes me a little happier. I try to take in the matches every other month or so if the drive isn't too far. I know my best years in professional wrestling are behind me, but I seriously feel that my best years as a writer are still ahead of me. I think that's an honest look at me.

I made a good living in wrestling. At one point it was a great living I dare say. I'm not a millionaire and I'm not rich, I'm comfortable where I'm at now, but I still have goals and writing more and more books is a big part of the next phase of my life. Who knows, I may even make a few dollars from my writing skills, but life is more than money. Being able to pay my bills, having something to eat, having a few friends, and healthy and happy children, well, I don't need much more than that. I can only live in one home, and I can only drive around in one car, and I have those things. Sure having a few dollars in my pocket is important to me but I don't need a whole lot more than what I've mentioned to keep me content and keep me happy. I got to experience things that many people only dream of doing and seeing through being in the wrestling business. I'll never forget where I came from and I know what a blessed life I've had. I owe most of that to wrestling. I'm not some old angry, bitter former wrestler pissed off that my wrestling career is over. As I mentioned, I'm excited about the next chapter of my life trying to become a writer. I got into wresting and I got out of it and moved on with my life, finally. So many others never have that chance to walk away. Believe me it's one of the most difficult battles many wrestlers face. But now, and I've said it before and I'll say it again, I'm finally using the wrestling business; the wrestling business isn't using me.

I'd like to add a little something that I feel is important. It was also in my last book, but I think it's important enough to once again add it in here as well. There are certain things that I have found that make my life worth living. I don't fear the judgment of others, nor do I judge others. It's not my place. I may question why people do certain things and of course I have my own opinions on things. I just choose not to be judgmental. If you judge people you don't have time to love people. I try to have love for life and for myself as well as for others as I find love is the single most important aspect of life. Spread love. Time spent with others, especially the ones you love is one of the best gifts you can give another.

Perseverance, keep on keeping on. Perseverance is the key to making it out of any hell you may be going through or help you reach any goals that you may have set for yourself. Just to merely exist on the planet is tough. Dare to dream and actually accomplish something worthwhile with your life, that's living, and that takes perseverance. Love, don't judge others, share your time wisely, and persevere.

Many people do good things but they only do them, conditionally. They try to capitalize on an opportunity to do good. They do good expecting something in return. The main reason they do these things is because they have a fear of going to hell or they have the desire of heaven. I neither fear nor seek either. These same people wouldn't necessarily still do these good deeds if there wasn't a hell or heaven. My personal belief is: I will try to do good because it's the right thing to do, not out of a fear or a desire. People like me are rare. I take great pride in knowing that at this point in my life, I have tried to do the right things for the right reasons.

We all make mistakes in life and I've made my share. Mistakes are different from regrets. With no regrets doesn't mean without any mistakes. Remember if you haven't made a mistake then you haven't ever really tried dong anything. Einstein said, "The only source of knowledge is experience." I decided at a young age to try to live or have as many

185

experiences as possible and to never regret anything. So far that's worked out pretty well. It's more about taking chances that others may not take. Our lives are really one big adventure in self-discovery. You can't expect a reward or to live a rewarding life if you're not willing to take chances at discovering yourself. How can you? Do it, and do it without regrets. Always learn from your mistakes, because there will be many. But, don't regret having tried doing something new. I'm alive and still have no regrets, that's really all I can say. No regrets! So without burning out, I'll just fade away. But, I'll do so with No Regrets!

"Non, je ne regrette rien."

"No, I regret nothing."

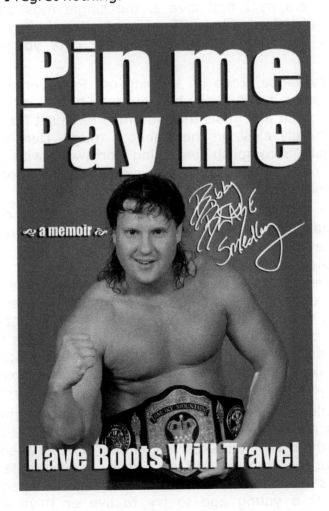

## ❧ Shameless Plugs ❧

Order your copy of Bobby's first book: *Pin Me Pay Me, Have Boots Will Travel* at:

http://www.amazon.com/Pin-Me-Pay-Boots-Travel/dp/1491248440/

I would be extremely grateful if you would be so kind as to post a fair and honest review on Amazon on any of my books. This address will take you directly to my Amazon author's page:

*http://www.amazon.com/Bobby-Blaze-Smedley/e/B00ETB3SBO*

## ❧ Contact Information ❧

amazon.com/author/bobbyblaze
Twitter: @bobbyblaze744
Instagram: bobbyblaze744
FaceBook: Bobby Blaze Smedley

## ❧ Special Thanks and Acknowledgments ❧

Jimm Smedley, Danny Phillips, Bobby Reynolds, Dave Selby, Matt Wolfe, Bill Bitner, Joe Blizzard, James Oliver, Dr. Bob Reynolds, Brady Smedley, Drake Smedley, Dean Malenko, Joe Malenko, Jim Cornette, Kevin Sullivan, DB Smedrock, Rick Newsome

## ❧ Special Photo Credits ❧

Zada Koury, Frank Shanly, Robin Litteral, Vanessa Stacy Wolfe, Kenny Wynn, Jody Simon, Mary Bond, Rick Newsome, Ken Jugan, and Tom Worden


Congratulations! You finished it!!! I hope you enjoyed my book. Again, I do appreciate your purchase.

## ❧ Just for Kicks ❧

*This is a bonus chapter for those of you who've stuck with me this far. Everything you've read so far has been true and accurate, to the best of my knowledge and ability. I'll let you be the judge from here on.*

## ❧ One Night in Knoxville ❧

One night after a wrestling show in Knoxville, I was hanging with the Rock–n–Roll Express. Those guys were really good to me. We were out at this club and having a good time. I was feeling pretty good kicking back a few cold ones.

Next thing I know Ricky and Robert had gone and I was there with this Tennessee chick I'd been dancing with all evening.

As we had a slow dance, I kept stepping on her feet. She just smiled at me and said, "You have big feet." I just nodded enjoying that sweet southern accent and the dance. Of course I kept stepping on her toes and feet as we danced. I know my boots had to be getting in her way as we danced. I told her I was sorry, but the cowboy boots were new and needed breaking in. She whispered in my ear, "It's okay baby," as she looked down at my feet. I was thinking the worst as I stepped off her foot. "It's ok honey, you know what they say don't ya?"

"No, not really!"

"Well, the girls in Tennessee all know that if a guy has big feet, he has a big thang."

"Thang?" I ask. "Yeah, you know, a big thang, like down there." She moaned in my ear as she was tugging around on my belt right there on the dance floor.

I was thinking to myself, "I might just get lucky tonight."

She came back to the room with me and let's just say I rocked her world Bobby MF'n Blaze style.

The next morning I woke up alone. I looked over and there was a $50 bill sitting right next to the lamp with a note. I thought, "Alright, performance went well, got lucky, had a good time and she even paid me. Life is good."

When I read the note reality sunk in about my "thang."
It said, "Buy some damn boots that fit."

## ๛ Goldberg and Me ๛

People often ask if I met Goldberg. Well yes I have, and I got to know him all too well. First off, he's a great guy. Very smart and articulate. Second, I wrestled him in Orlando, FL and was "victim number 67." Let me further add that when he speared me right before his big finishing "jackhammer suplex" he basically speared me right out of my boots. Great guy I tell ya.

Never let the truth stand in the way of a good yarn, I always say, so, I got to know him outside the ring as well. I mean he's a guy who played "The Hammer" in the remake of *The Longest Yard*. As one gym owner said when Goldberg walked into a gym to work out before a pay-per-view show, "Goldberg, The biggest Jew since Moses."

One time we were sharing a room when a knock came on our hotel room door. We answered it and two of the hottest chicks I'd ever seen were standing there. They were stacked and packed. Damn! Well, Goldberg tells them he has to get some sleep so he can hit the gym in the morning and also get ready for a match. He took the business way too seriously. He always ate right, trained right, and got the proper rest required to be a complete professional athlete. I always have had a lot of respect for him in and outside the ring. He was always very professional around me and in the locker room.

I thought to myself, "I'll never get a chance with a hot chick like that ever again, let alone two of them." Well the ladies left a little frustrated but understood. "Marks and rats, ugh," I thought to myself. Well needless to say I could hardly sleep that night. And when I did fall asleep I awoke with the biggest hard-on in my hand I've have had since I was 15. Damn! That cock was harder than Chinese Algebra. So, I got to thinking, "I've got to go next door where these super-fine hot babes were staying." Also thinking I probably shouldn't wake up Goldberg, I'd just sneak out real quiet like, and he would be none the wiser come morning. As I was creeping towards the door, I noticed this huge figure right behind me.

"Um, hey, Goldberg, I was just going next door, I just couldn't stand it any longer. I've got to have one of those ladies. I'm so horny, and besides, I've got one of the biggest, hardest, hard-ons I've had in years." He just grunted, and continued to walk close behind me. Turning slowly, I asked him where he was going. He said, "I'm going with you, cause that's my dick you got in your hand." Oh well, yes I know Goldberg!

## ⊰ Fromunda Cheese ⊱

One night after a CPW show near Cincinnati, a car load of us stopped at an all-night truck stop. We went to the sandwich or deli side to order something to go. "Buzzsaw" Jones asked the lady behind the counter if he could get some "fromunda cheese" on his sandwich. She told him that she didn't think they had any, and then made the dreadful mistake of saying she had never heard of it and said "What kind of cheese it?" Buzzsaw told her it was a fine Italian cheese and was surprised that being in the sandwich business at a truck stop she had never heard of it.

Again, she asked, "What kinda cheese is it and where does it come from?" To which he responded, "It's called 'fromunda cheese,' and comes from unda my nuts!" Man, we all just fell about the place in laughter. It was just one of those moments you had to be there to truly appreciate. I'd say all of our sandwiches had spit on them that night.

## ⊰ Sports Reporter ⊱

I can't believe that a sports and entertainment reporter was interviewing me, when right in the middle of the interview, he said to me, "Do you know who my five favorite famous people from Kentucky are, Bobby Blaze?" I said, "No, who are they?" That reporter said, "Muhammad Ali, Adolph Rupp, George Clooney, Johnny Depp, and..." I said, "Don't go any further! And me, Bobby Blaze." And this reporter said, "Why no, Billy Ray Cyrus!" "Billy Ray Cyrus?" I drew back and knocked him on his ass!

Special thank you or with apologies to Terry Funk for the idea. It was just too funny to resist Terry.

190

## ⮟ Sexco ⮞

One day, my brother Jimm and I were riding down route 23, you know the good old, "Country Music Highway" trying to make a town down near Pikeville, Kentucky. This is back when there was some little two-lane sections of it. So anyway, we're just riding along and I come up on this curvy part of the road, not that's there's many straight sections of it, and out of nowhere, there's a big gasoline truck parked by a local service station. Now seeing a coal truck or a hundred or so isn't that big of a deal on 23. Seeing an oil rig or gasoline truck isn't that unusual either, but this one was different. This one however was one like I've never seen before or since. It was baby blue, and appeared to be longer than most trucks. It was polished with what looked like a fresh coat of paint or at least had been recently waxed and on the side of that truck in big black letters was, "SEXCO." I just turned to my brother and without batting an eye; I said to him, "That's some good fucking gas right there." Man, he just started laughing his ass off at my simply sophomoric observation, and we must have laughed about that all the way to the next town. It was just that funny. We still laugh about it today. "SEXCO, Good Fucking Gas!"

## ⮟ The Pretzel Hold ⮞

Having traveled the world over and wrestling and sometimes really fighting guys from other countries one has to be able to protect himself at all times. Sometimes in wrestling some promoters will put a guy in the ring with you, knowing that he is the best wrestler and fighter he has. So he puts his guy in there to protect his version of the belt or his territory or in this case his promotion. This is so someone from the opposition doesn't come in and beat his champ. I was in this situation on more than one occasion.

I was traveling overseas to England for a tournament that would have wrestlers representing several countries, including England, South Africa, Japan, Germany, the US and the USSR. Many of these countries still have their matches take place in rounds much like boxing does. That was the layout for these matches. I was scheduled for three rounds consisting of five minutes each. In my first match I was scheduled to face a big guy who reminded me of Ivan Drago, the big fighter from Russia in the *Rocky IV* movie. Only this guy was a little bigger at 6-foot-8 and 275 pounds, and a whole lot uglier.

This guy's name was also Ivan. Over the loud speaker, it was hard to understand at first, but I did gather his first name was Ivan. I think it was Ivan Knockertitsoff or something like that.

Anyway, each wrestler had a trainer, a corner man, and an interpreter in their corner to cut down on any confusion that might take place during the fight and also to help each wrestler between rounds. The promoters really did this tournament up right. My trainer told me to just do my best, try to win one of the first two rounds and then make it into the third and final round so we could, "Give a good show kid, and then get the hell out of here with our payoffs."

The first round went pretty smoothly but it was obvious Ivan was a very accomplished wrestler but he wasn't nearly as polished as I was a pro. Most of his moves where quick and effective take downs and holds that I had to counter in order to avoid being pinned in the first round, the round I was "scheduled to win" before moving on to round two.

In between rounds, the interpreter told my corner man and trainer to, "Avoid Ivan's 'Pretzel Hold' at all cost. No man has ever escaped it." It was rumored to be an extremely painful hold if he were to get me in it. Now I had no idea what the hell this pretzel hold was and really didn't want to find out. I was there to work my match, put him over in the second and third rounds, and collect my payoff and move on to the next town. But, in all fairness, I wasn't just going to let this guy steamroll over me even if he was one big ugly intimidating guy. Well, it was all I could do to keep him off me in round two. Needless to say, I was knocked groggy by the end of it.

Splashing my face with cold water, my corner man said I was doing great, my trainer told me to take him to the mat and try to hold him down until the last minute or so of the fight then go into the finish. The foreign interpreter had a look of concern on his face and was mumbling, "The pretzel hold, the pretzel hold, avoid it Bobby, avoid it."

When round three started, everyone in the capacity crowd was on their feet and really into the match. Even though I was dazed I could clearly hear, "Round three! Round three!" followed by the sound of the bell. Ivan came out of his corner and immediately was all over me. It was all I could do on wobbly legs to not only try to keep him off me, but to try to counter and escape every hold he tried to grab me with. This was becoming more frequent and difficult as the round progressed. And then out of nowhere, I was in a hold I had never been in before or since. "This is it I bet, 'the dreaded pretzel hold.'"

I continued to battle, struggling, trying my hardest to escape this hold. I was indeed tied up like the knot in a pretzel. I knew I was supposed to put this guy over in the third and final round, just like I had agreed to in the second, but there was no way I was going to tap out of some hold I'd never been in before, besides that, I couldn't even move my arms and hands enough to tap out if I wanted to.

Bam! Boom! Kapow! And a bunch of other word overlays were all that could be heard from the ring. There was disbelief throughout the arena as to what the fans were witnessing. And the next thing you know I was standing in the middle of the ring and getting my hand raised in victory. My trainer was smiling from the corner. Ivan Knockertitsoff was lying over in his corner with a look of confusion. The interpreter was up in the ring with me as the ring announcer asked me a series of questions in a cross between broken English and Russian.

"Well Bobby Blaze, not only did you win the match, but you have become the first and only man to ever escape the pretzel hold. How in the world did you ever escape such a hold?" After the interpreter repeated the question, I calmly looked around the sold out building, looked straight into the television camera and said, "When he had me in that pretzel hold I couldn't move anything. I knew I was doomed. I was about to be defeated. I was in pain and wanted to quit so bad. I knew that there was no escaping this maneuver. Just when I thought I could take no more, I looked up and saw two big ol' hairy balls hanging right down in my face. And let me tell you, a man doesn't know his own strength until he bites his own nuts!" The Pretzel Hold!!!

Lightning Source UK Ltd.
Milton Keynes UK
UKHW021912021118
331678UK00019B/559/P